SETTING UP AND MAINTAINING AN EFFECTIVE PRIVATE PRACTICE

A practical workbook for
mental health practitioners

Psychology, Psychotherapy and Counselling

SETTING UP AND MAINTAINING AN EFFECTIVE PRIVATE PRACTICE

A practical workbook for
mental health practitioners

with access to resources section on
<www.karnacbooks.com>
for financial spreadsheets and useful information

Philippa Weitz BEd, MSc

KARNAC
LONDON   NEW YORK

First published in 2006 by
H. Karnac (Books) Ltd.
6 Pembroke Buildings, London NW10 6RE

British Library Cataloguing in Publication Data
A C.I.P. for this book is available from the British Library

ISBN10: 1 85575 425 8
ISBN13: 978 1 85575 425 6

Typeset by RefineCatch Limited, Bungay, Suffolk
Printed in Great Britain

www.karnacbooks.com

CONTENTS

ACKNOWLEDGEMENTS

With grateful thanks to Robin Wilson, of Wilson Sandford and Co, Chartered Accountants at 85 Church Road, Hove (Tel. 01273 821 441) and Member of the UK200 Group, for proof-reading the financial aspects of the book.

This is also proof of the value of networking as Robin and I are members of the same Rotary Club.

Use of terminology

I use a number of different ways of describing the therapist in this book—the book is equally suitable for all those developing a psychological therapies private practice—including counsellors, psychotherapists, psychologists, psychiatrists and many others, please do not feel excluded—if you are planning a private practice, or already run one but want to improve what you do— this book is for you.

INTRODUCTION

Training as a counsellor or psychotherapist is rarely a first training. Most of us, for a wide variety of reasons, train as counsellors or psychotherapists as a second career. You may have been in business and therefore already have good business management skills, or you may have been in a wide variety of professions where business skills and knowledge was not so necessary.

This book is aimed at those of you with less business skills and knowledge and aims to provide you with enough competence to develop a thriving private practice.

All business involve risk-taking—this book will help you to work out whether you are cut out for the risks involved in managing a private practice. Throughout the book there will be question and answer sections which are designed for you to analyse your motives for wanting to set up a business, and to assess the skills and knowledge that you have, as well as providing pointers as to where you can go and get more advice and training for certain skills. You wouldn't dream of not continuing your Continuing Professional Development as a therapist, so why not in the business world as well. And the good news is you can offset it against tax.

Let's move on to our first examples of practitioners launching their own practice. We are going to use Donna and Simon as our examples. Please get to know these characters, think about people you know that Donna or Simon remind you of, and think about these two, Donna and Simon, as you read on through the book and see how what the book teaches could have improved their business success (or failure).

Example 1—Donna

Donna was a Chief Inspector in the Police Force. She took early retirement and did a Masters in Psychotherapy. The course was an excellent course on the theory, research and practice of counselling, but it did not prepare her for the real world of work. Once qualified, she realised her options were limited in getting paid work and she combined with three of her course colleagues, Jane (formerly a nurse), Susan (formerly a probation officer) and John (formerly a prison officer) to form a new practice. They had all graduated at the same time and none of them had any experience of running a business. In addition, none of them did a business start-up course. With little advice they formed a partnership, hired an office suite in the West End of London with a 5-year lease, paying a rent of £30,000 a year, exclusive of all costs such as business rates and utilities. They opened a bank account with one of the Big Four and used that bank's very excellent business CD to go on and prepare a very comprehensive business plan for their practice. They made one serious mistake: they had been over-ambitious on the number of clients they would get in the first year. Susan decided to drop out after 6 months because the stress of the worry made her ill, leaving the others "holding the baby".

Nine months later the other three realised that they were not going to make it—they were left with debts totalling £18,000 each and a very sour taste of failure in their mouths.

Donna found this particularly difficulty to accept since she had never been in this position before, either financially or professionally, and completely gave up counselling as a result.

Example 2—Simon

Simon qualified as a counsellor whilst continuing to teach part-time. After completing his 4-year generic training he took an additional course specialising in working with children. Once qualified, he decided to continue teaching whilst starting a private practice. He had an office at home at the bottom of the garden that he used for some tutoring and it was easy for him to adapt this to a counselling room. Within 3 months he had five clients, which he felt was enough for him at that stage. Alone five clients would not have paid all his living expenses but was a useful source of income. Spreading his financial risk meant that he could pursue his counselling work slowly and develop his private practice. His teaching took a lot of his time and did not leave him with much mental or physical capacity to develop a new business. At some stage he would need to make some decisions about the directions he might want to move in if he ever wanted to do more than sit on the fringe of the counselling profession.

I want to start by being brutal: counsellors often have a difficulty in developing a business plan because they are caring individuals (this is often what has drawn you to counselling in the first place)—and don't like seeing what they do as the same as selling widgets—please bear with me while I expand this theme in this book and demonstrate how important business planning is—even for a part-time private practice.

It is very common for those of us in the counselling world to have more than one job—counselling work is not always easy to get and is rarely full time. Indeed, many of us will always have to split our working lives between counselling and another profession. This can create many tensions for us, and certainly reduces the amount of time that we have available—as two part-time jobs usually seem to create more work than one full-time job. This can have an effect on our families, our personal life and how much we can give to each job and even our ability to be effective.

Good counselling and psychotherapy courses struggle to get everything into a course in an attempt to provide their students with the necessary theory, research and practical skills to practise competently after graduation. Few courses delve deeply into how you are to practise afterwards or even provide you with the necessary training. However, when you ask most students how they are thinking of using their training afterwards a sizeable majority usually think they will do some private work—to do some private work is to run a practice, in other words, a business, with all the responsibilities that this involves—even for one client!

This book will not answer every question, and cannot deal with every situation. Continuously changing law and policy changes mean that you must check points of information and law and how they refer to your situation.

My aim to is provide a framework for those who are starting out and may choose to work either full- or part-time in private practice. This book should try to help you avoid some of the pitfalls that I fell into—and a few more.

It seems so easy to start a private practice—you pick up a couple of private clients, see them at home in the evening, take their payments, keep a few notes and, *voilà*, you have a private practice. Such an unthought-out beginning is fraught with potential problems and is not good enough.

Going on a course on setting up a private practice, or getting someone to mentor you and advise you will always be a much better solution that reading my two-dimensional words—but these options are not open to everyone.

This book is not the definitive book on setting up a private counselling or psychotherapy practice—a business—you will find many "Setting up a business" books in the bookshops, but at least 50% of what is written in them is irrelevant to you as a counsellor or psychotherapist—the problem for you is knowing which 50%! This book will give you the essentials—if you want more you will need to research further.

This book will be out of date as soon as it appears—the law is constantly changing. I cannot take responsibility for your actions as a result of reading this book and I urge you to always take professional advice—it is never wasted.

Finally, choosing a good training, engaging in your own personal development and reflection, belonging to a reputable professional organization, adhering to the necessary codes of ethics, engaging in serious and competent supervision for the context you are working in, undertaking continuing professional development are all different aspects of the profession you have chosen: caring for the psychological welfare of the general public. In private practice where you will be less well supported, and far more isolated, it is very important to ensure that you always aim for the highest levels of competence and care.

CHECKING YOUR MOTIVATION FOR SETTING UP A PRIVATE PRACTICE

It's OK to need to earn money. Counsellors are often embarrassed about this and feel it gets in the way of their caring. If you don't sort this out in your head you will be useless in private practice.

A counselling business is one of a group of professional businesses that earns its money from the fees it charges, rather like a solicitor or an accountant. It doesn't usually have items for sale like the books in W.H. Smith.

For those in the people business it is very important to view the minutes and hours you work as opportunities to earn income. You will need to view each of your counselling hours as one potential unit of income. As a one-man band you will be limited in minutes and hours that you have available and will need to think very hard about your priorities and what is important to you and what is important to the business as there are only so many hours in a week. There will be other ways you can increase your income, but that is jumping ahead!

When teaching about setting up a private practice I call the hourly units available for working in a week widgets—your business is no different from the toy maker that needs to make 450 toys a week to break even—that's his bottom line. You will need to work ouT your bottom line—that's what working through this book will show you.

Some tough talking!

I need you to take this idea seriously as being a therapist in private practice MUST have the same business aims as say an accountant or a garage owner—your aim is to make a PROFIT. If this type of conversation is not for you please put this book back on the shelf and know that you have already answered the first question and answer section below and that private practice is not for you.

Let's be clear, if you don't make a profit you will go bust—and that is very, very unpleasant and entirely avoidable.

Running a private practice will have dual, sometimes conflicting, aims:

- To care for your clients' mental health
- To make money

You need to be sure that you are comfortable with combining these two aims—if not, private practice is not for you.

Workbook Question and Answer Session:
Do I see my clients' hours as units for sale?

Do I look at these hours/units objectively as a point of departure in my business planning?

If the answer to either of these questions is "no" then please read on but private practice may not be for you—it is not for everyone. If it is yes—that's a good start.

Distinguish between you as a practitioner and the practice as a business. They are two separate entities.

Most of us make the mistake of pushing ourselves rather than our business identity. Try to see the two as completely separate, even down to giving the practice an objective name such as The Elms Counselling Centre. This will help you to keep some objectivity between yourself and the business you run and help you realise that *you are not the business*. We will return to this theme in Chapter One.

Try not to let the large number of things you have to do to create and maintain a successful business prevent you from starting out. If you can afford it, buy in the specialist skills that you don't have (e.g. 2 hours book-keeping a month), at least until you have become more skilled. We will return to this theme in Chapters Two and Three.

If you reach a section in the book which you simply become too phobic over (like me and accounts) then ask a professional to help you to take care of that part of the business. It will do you NO GOOD AT ALL to stuff all the accounts back under the bed in a shoebox and hope they will go away. It gets worse if you do that—believe me.

Learning to run a business takes years and many people take professional qualifications to do so—you will suddenly be your own accountant, lawyer, financial adviser and toilet cleaner all rolled into one. And all you wanted to do was see clients!

One last thing—about personal safety—a private small practice is a far more dangerous place to practise than a group practice, working within a corporate or NHS setting. Your isolation makes you vulnerable and you need to take this very seriously—we will return to this theme in Chapter Four.

HOW TO USE THIS BOOK

Do not feel that you need to read every page of this book—it will only be a good cure for insomnia.

Suggestion 1

Select the chapter that seems most necessary and start there. You do not need to read the chapters in any particular order, although there is some cross-referencing as things can be both legal and financial, for example.

Whatever you do please try not to panic when you don't understand something—go and find someone who can help you understand it.

Suggestion 2

Treat this work as a work-book and make it your own. Make notes as you go and use a highlighter to link your notes and the printed notes.

Use a pencil to fill in the Question and Answer sections so that as you develop your ideas you can go back and change some of your original answers—you will find that your ideas change and develop as you go through your learning.

CHAPTER ONE

Marketing

Getting your first clients—telling the world about your business

"No clients, no business"

I n this section I shall look at how you can get clients, because without clients you have no business. *This was where Donna and her colleagues took a wrong turn.*

It is always getting your foot on the first rung, getting the first clients, that is so difficult. No one knows who you are, you have not built up a reputation, and there is plenty of competition.

Let's dive in and start finding you clients. There is quite a lot to think about in order to achieve that.

1.1 Marketing and advertising

1.1.1 Marketing—getting yourself known

Marketing is a broader word than advertising. This is about how you get yourself known and gain (and retain) your professional reputation as a counsellor.

1.1.2 Setting short- and long-term goals

Workbook Question and Answer Session:

What are the major long-term goals for my private practice that I wish to achieve over a 5-year period?

How am I going to achieve these long-term goals?

What are my immediate short-term goals that I wish to achieve within my first year?

How am I going to achieve these short-term goals?

If you can decide on what you want from your business, your goals, then you will know better how to market yourself. Think about Donna's and Simon's goals which were quite different, some were more achievable than others. Think about setting realistic goals. As these are your first serious questions you are likely to change your mind about your short- and long-term goals when you have gone further through your reading and planning, so you may wish to revisit these again.

1.1.3 Deciding what is unique about your business

In the jargon—you need to decide what is your "USP"—your unique selling proposition. Do I sense some of you getting a bit phobic suddenly!? This is just the sort of language to turn me off. In plain English what you do need to decide is what you have to offer, and how it is different to any of your competitors. I suggest you start your answer on rough paper as this exercise is not that easy and you will have a few false starts.

Example

Simon was the only qualified child counsellor in a 50-mile radius; this would give him an edge over others for working with children. Donna's group ignored their combined training, skills and experience in the police, probation service and prison service as they might have been well placed to think about taking some additional training and developing work in those sectors where they are already known.

Starting to answer these questions will lead you to think not only what is unique about your practice but also about how you can adapt your previous work to the current context by bolting on some additional training.

Workbook Question and Answer Session:

1. *What is unique about my private practice?*

2. *How can I sum this up in no more than 10 words?*

1.1.4 Soul searching questions

Three questions that you must ask yourself before you set out in business, and answer in detail are:

Workbook Question and Answer Session:

What service can I (my practice) offer?

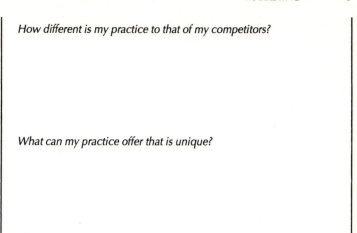

How different is my practice to that of my competitors?

What can my practice offer that is unique?

The answer to these three questions will determine how you develop your practice/business and will form the basis of all your marketing and will underpin your business.

As a result of this exercise you may come up with a short phrase that you want as part of your logo—this is called a USP. Have a look at correspondence from other companies and you will start to notice that a number include a USP. If you think it is over the top, then leave it, it is certainly not essential for a professional clinician. What is important is that you think about it.

Workbook Question and Answer Session:

What is my USP?

Workbook Question and Answer Session:

Do I need to get any additional training, or to buy in specialist skills, to equip me for achieving my goals?

1.1.5 Deciding on your marketing strategy

Once you have decided on your major goals and your USP there are some more general questions you may need to ask yourself before you can start to put together your business plan and marketing strategy:

Workbook Question and Answer Session:

Does the business need to support me full time?

Do I want to develop a big and well-known practice? How ambitious am I?

Do I want to be known for my academic interests and join the conference circuit etc.?

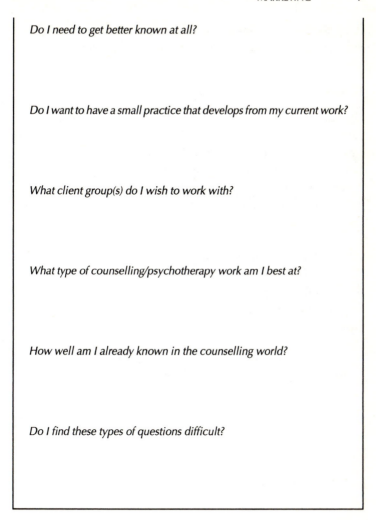

Do I need to get better known at all?

Do I want to have a small practice that develops from my current work?

What client group(s) do I wish to work with?

What type of counselling/psychotherapy work am I best at?

How well am I already known in the counselling world?

Do I find these types of questions difficult?

Whatever the answers to these and the other questions you ask yourself, the answers will be quite unique according to your strengths and weaknesses. Be ruthlessly honest about both as these will help you to decide whether to proceed with setting up a private practice and what hurdles you might need to overcome along the way. At any point during these questions you may decide that private practice is not for you. It is not for everyone.

1.1.6 The ultimate goal in marketing

The ideal goal for the development of your business, from a marketing point of view, will be to develop your professional reputation and competence to such an extent that you do not need to undertake any additional marketing.

Meanwhile the rest of us have to use marketing as a means of getting ourselves known!

1.2 The target for your marketing

First of all you need to decide to whom you are advertising your services. You will probably need to inform the following groups—how will you do this?

Workbook Question and Answer Session:

- *The general public*   *HOW?*

- *Your counselling colleagues*   *HOW?*

- *Associated professions such as psychologists, psychiatrists, GPs, etc.*   *HOW?*

1.2.1 The general public

On the whole the general public has little awareness of the true nature of counselling, psychotherapy, psychology or psychiatry, or understands the differences between each if these professional disciplines. Consequently there are many myths flying around that are generally unhelpful for you when you are looking for clients as there can be a severe mismatch. They have also no idea what are valid qualifications or who might be a good practitioner. You are about to be an ambassador for your profession with that client—you need to get it right for their sake and make spot on decisions about who to accept and who not to accept for private counselling. Good assessment, as in other sectors of the counselling industry, remains one of the cornerstones of good practice. If you are not experienced in assessment this might need to be one of the first areas that you invest in, for your continuing professional development.

The man in the street in distress looking for help may take one of several possible lines of action:

- They will go to see their GP (see the section below regarding GPs).
- They will look in Yellow Pages, yell.com or Thompson's Directory
- They will ring the British Association for Counselling and Psychotherapy (BACP) or the United Kingdom Council for Psychotherapy (UKCP) and will be given names from the BACP or UKCP directory (BACP and UKCP are not the only organisations—there are other professional organisations).
- They will ring The Samaritans, the Citizens Advice Bureau or other self-help organisation.
- They will ask a friend who they know has been in counselling for a recommendation.
- They will search the internet.

Through one of the above routes you may receive your client: my experience is that all the above can lead to inappropriate referrals (there is no perfect referral source in private practice, but assessment will help you select who is most suitable for private counselling help).

Example

One of the first private clients Joanna received from a GP referral set fire to her house and threatened to be violent to her. She was poorly supervised (what did she not tell her supervisor?!) and should never have accepted this client in the first place as she was well beyond the limits of her competence and needed specialist care in an appropriate setting—not her home.

This brings me to mention areas that have nothing to do with marketing, but must be the first consequence of successful advertising.

Workbook Question and Answer Session:

What is your assessment procedure and how appropriate is the referral?

What safe setting have you created for seeing clients?

The above box does not really do justice to the space needed for these answers and you may need to use spare paper. All these issues will come out at later stages of this book, but I would immediately ask you to start thinking about them.

1.2.2 Your counselling and psychotherapy colleagues

You will find it useful to network with your professional colleagues, but be aware, they are at the same time both your potential source of referral AND your competition. Remember, to be successful in business, you must have no room for sentiment and if you are the new boy or new girl on the block you may engender hostility and jealousy—just be ready for it and think about how you will deal with this before it actually happens.

Referrals between colleagues are very common for at least three reasons:

- Your colleague has no spaces
- Your colleague feels that he/she is an inappropriate person to work with this particular client (for example, a counsellor who has experienced an eating disorder may prefer not to work with this group of clients).
- A colleague may suddenly be unable to work, either through illness, holiday or death.

The advantage of getting a client via referral is that you should receive some information about the client even before meeting them which will enable you to decide if they are suitable to be seen in your private practice. Just be aware that sometimes a client is referred on because there is some difficulty. Make sure you have the full information before taking on a referral as referrals and transfers of clients can be very distressing for the client and the transition needs to be well managed.

On the subject of referrals, many of your clients will self-refer—this too will lead to problems as you may not be told anything near the whole picture.

The organisation you trained with may well be able to provide you with referrals.

Whatever the route, the key to the successful beginning of a counselling process and relationship will be assessment.

1.2.3 Associated professions such as psychologists, psychiatrists, GPs

One of the most important things for you to do in private practice will be for you to gain a positive reputation with your NHS colleagues locally. Indeed it goes beyond this, as you will need to consult with and refer on to these professional colleagues in counselling, psychology, psychotherapy, psychiatry, social work and general practice.

Time spent doing this will reap many rewards and may lead to referrals once you have developed your reputation. GPs may have a counsellor attached to the practice, but may not. With the current changes in general practice all this may change.

Once you have worked out your list you will want to write to these individuals and organisations to introduce yourself and do everything and anything you can to get known by them.

Workbook Question and Answer Session:

Who are the professionals that I need to network with?

Psychiatrists

General Practitioners

Social Services

Psychologists

Counsellors and Psychotherapists

Voluntary Organisations (e.g. MIND)

Other

1.3 How you make yourself known to your public

Example

An English osteopath recently moved to the South of France and set up a new practice. The other local osteopaths showed great jealousy to her arrival. In addition, she didn't have the right to advertise. This did not stop her—she set up a pilates class locally so that people would get to know her, and gradually set up a support group with an older group of osteopaths near to retirement who were not threatened by her arrival. Within 6 months she began to be accepted.

This example is given to encourage you to think creatively about how you can make yourself known to "your public", as you may already have some stiff competition from other counsellors who will not be pleased to see a newcomer.

Having discussed some possible avenues for looking for clients what practically can you do to get yourself known?

1.3.1 Reputation

The first and most important area to develop, as I have already said, is to develop your reputation as a well-trained, effective and successful counsellor.

1.3.2 Putting together a leaflet/flyer

Having decided which particular group of clients you want to work with (e.g. drug dependence, bereavement) put together a brief summary about your practice and the services it offers. "Brief" will depend on whom you are targeting.

General public   If you are writing a flyer for the general public, make sure you use words that they understand—interpersonal skills, transference, psychodynamic psychotherapy may be words that a professional would understand, but you will have lost most of your target audience, and along with that your potential clients.

Professionals   If you are writing for doctors they like things to be short but technically correct. Remember though that a GP is trained in a wide variety of medical specialisms that enabled him to correctly assess and diagnose—but he may have had very little training in psychotherapy and counselling and may also not understand specific words used technically in counselling and psychotherapy, such as "supervision".

You may need to write different leaflets for different target groups.

Workbook Question and Answer Session:

Writing your flyer: Remember though, be short and clear and make sure that you include all necessary information such as:

- *Name of the practice*
- *Contact name*
- *Contact number*
- *Contact address*
- *A brief description about the practice*
- *How to get to the practice*
- *A brief description about the (different) treatments available*
- *A brief description of the conditions that you treat—remain fairly general otherwise someone will say "Oh, they don't do . . ."*
- *Any qualifications and accreditation that the practice and its members is eligible to list.*

You need to ensure that you use font styles and sizes that are easy to read and large enough. Keep it simple, do not use more than two fonts in your flyer. If you are not sure what I mean go and stand outside the local newsagents and read the small ad cards. Which ones are the easiest to read? Why do some work better than others?

Once you have prepared your flyer show it to other people, particular those whom you know will be honest—put the flyer 30 feet away from them and see if they can read it—that's the equivalent of the length of a large waiting room—you often only get one hit at telling people about your services—make sure it is very, very obvious.

Do not make unrealistic claims as these could be held against you later.

1.3.3 Choosing a name

I know it sounds grandiose, but remember you are promoting far more than yourself, you are promoting a sound business that may grow. Talking about "John Smith" as opposed to "John Smith Associates" leaves no room for growth and change.

The name you give your practice will give everyone a message. If you choose a name like "The Cedars Counselling Practice" it gives me the idea that it has been named after a house or some trees or a location—but it is at least neutral. "The Good Listener Practice" would make me nearly ill and I would probably not choose to ring that one! "John Smith Associates" gives me the idea that there is more than one practitioner in the practice and that John Smith is the most important person in the practice. Do not use initials such as J.S. Associates.

Think carefully about whether to use your name in the practice name. It is very common if you are buying a limited company to choose a name such as John Smith Associates precisely because there is no John Smith.

If you choose your name and things go wrong you can never get away from your trading and personal names. Even worse, I know of a business in a related field where the individuals concerned cannot trade under their own name as they sold their business to a competitor. A little while later they decided to start up all over again as things did not work out well for them with their new business partners. So the general advice is to keep away from trading under your own name.

You will also need to be careful to choose a unique practice name. There is no national register that you can apply to and the regulations are different if you are choosing to practice as a sole trader/partnership or if you set up/purchase a limited company (I will discuss the difference between these in a later chapter).

If you set up or buy a **limited company** it is fairly straight-forward—you cannot have the same name as any other com-pany—Companies House will not allow you to register it. You are also not allowed to use certain words, for example: royal, British, National and English. You will need to check with Companies House before making a decision.

For **sole traders** and **partnerships** it is more tricky. The most important thing is to make sure that you do not "trade off" anyone else's name. For example, to be a bit over obvious, if you set up a food business and call it Fortnum and Mason, they could take you to court for "trading off" their name. Try to stay away from any nationally known organisation and look up the name you wish to choose in all the local telephone directories and Thompson's directories, and any other sources you can think of, especially the internet (do a search under Google). For example, you will find hundreds of "Red Lion" pubs, but they are scattered all over the country and therefore not likely to affect each other's business. But if there was a chain of Red Lion pubs that specialised in a particular theme, and you decided to set up a pub and name it Red Lion and have the same theme, then you would be opening yourself to the accusation of "trading off".

1.3.4 Networking

One of the best ways of getting your reputation known is via networking. This has an added advantage that you may not have experienced yet—working in private practice can be very isolating. Join your local BACP, UKCP (and other) specialist interest groups and other local interest networks.

Joining the Institute of Directors, the Rotary Club, the Federation of Small Businesses are examples of ways in which you can broaden your network. Going to business breakfasts and lunches are excellent ways of networking both informally and formally. You usually get your 3 minutes to say who are you and what you do—make the most of it and don't forget to take business cards everywhere you go! Prepare before you go, make a few notes and take some literature and business cards with you. Be ruthless and shameless in this form of advertising as it is relatively free and depends on how you can present yourself.

1.3.5 Direct advertising

This is a tricky area and can be like tearing up pound notes! My rule of thumb is not to spend a fortune, as it generally does not pay. Make a list of where you want to advertise, decide on an annual budget and stick to it. Direct contact is a far more effective way of creating a client base.

There are a number of methods of advertising that you may want to consider, though you should remember my words of caution about the general public and self-referral.

You will need to consider one or some of the following:

Workbook Question and Answer Session:

What is my annual budget for direct advertising?

Mailshot   *Fairly effective if directly targeted—think about your style of writing and clarity of presentation. Who will I target?*

Newspapers   *Very expensive, and the returns will not be very good, also you will get some very inappropriate clients—you could try and get some editorial cover—quite a lot of local newspapers run a weekly feature on local businesses. You may be asked to place an advert in return for the editorial space.*

Which newspapers would be suitable? How much do they charge for an ad?

Flyers   *Try distributing your flyers to local general practices (obviously with the permission of the GP practice) and other mental health centres, self-help, psychology services, osteopaths, homeopaths, dentists etc. Don't forget to get permission first. Also, such methods will be far more effective if you have got to know the clinicians in these centres who may on occasions give your leaflets to appropriate people. Remember, despite the Sainsbury Centre for Mental Health and Lord Layard suggestions about the need to treat the "silent majority" with mental health needs, the NHS is very limited in its resources and cannot see everyone—this is one of your trump cards.*

Go back to the list of professionals you made earlier and see if you can think of anyone else to add to this list.

Directories   *Yell.com, Yellow Pages and Thompson's directories are useful places to be listed—the downside is that this information is available to EVERYONE. If you are using a home phone number, could this cause a problem.*

Website   *You might wish to set up a simple website—again—keep it simple. If you do not have the skills to build your own website do not allow others to talk you into spending hundreds of pounds on a website—you should be able to get a very acceptable straight-forward website for between £150 and £400, depending on how complicated the design and content is. Ensure that appropriate search words are included to draw people to your website.*

Professional associations   *Ensure you are listed in the professional organisation's directories appropriate to you—BACP and UKCP have directories. You may belong to other professional organisations—make sure you are on their lists that they give out to enquirers. Such lists are then passed down to other organisations such as Citizens Advice Bureaux—I recently received a client this way.*

1.3.6 The "look" you give your business

The image you give your practice will influence who comes to you and what they think of you. This is important in a number of areas:

1.3.6.1 Presentation of material

Have you got a logo? A logo gives people the idea that you are an established business. A logo need not be complicated or expensive. I know of at least one international company whose logo was decided by a small group having one discussion and it has been very successful. Do not ask a PR company to design a logo and "look" for you unless you can really afford it. You will have your own ideas—just keep doodling and something will come out of it eventually. Please note, a logo is not essential and if nothing jumps out at you then leave it. The best logos are simple but giving a strong message.

Stationery This is very important and also gives a strong message. If you create headed paper on your computer and print it out yourself it may look amateurish—depending on your designing abilities, the quality of the paper and how good your printer is. Alternatively ask around about good printers and get two quotations for how much it will cost. Do not be afraid to shop around, prices vary enormously between different companies for the same service. They will be able to tidy up your designs and prepare your printing for you.

Workbook Question and Answer Session: you may need to do lots of doodling on separate paper for this section—just put the results in here.

Planning my logo—what might be important elements?

What look do I want for all my stationery and flyers?

1.3.6.2 Stationery you will need

- Business cards (250)
- A4 letterheads (1,000)—these could be done on your computer as a Word template if you have a good quality printer.
- A4 continuation sheets (possibly with your logo on them, but not the full details as on the front sheet). These are very useful for report writing. The logo on continuation sheets makes your stationery easily identifiable even through the fax machine.
- Your leaflets (500—2,000). Do not print too many, they get out of date too quickly.
- Appointment cards (1,000)—these could be doubled up with your business cards. Ask for the appointment details (and brief Terms and Conditions—particularly cancellation arrangements) to be printed on the back.

The main thing to remember about printing is that the difference for printing 250, 500 and 1,000 is very little. Most of the charges will be for the design, plate making and setting up. The paper itself and the machine time will add very little cost if you have extras printed at the same time. It is far more expensive to print two lots of 250 cards, for example, on two separate occasions, than to print 500 cards in one go.

However, you need to get a balance between what you think you can use before it gets out of date, what you will need and the cost.

Shop around before you decide on a printer—also you may be able to generate a lot of your materials on the computer if you are computer-literate—but if you are not, please get things printed properly as amateur looking cards, headed paper and flyers look just that, amateur, and will give the wrong message about the quality of your work.

Workbook Items to Order:

To order	Stationery Item	Amount
Yes/No	Business cards	
Yes/No	A4 letterheads	
Yes/No	A4 continuation sheets	
Yes/No	Your leaflets	
Yes/No	Appointment cards	

1.3.6.3 *What to include on your stationery:*

- Name of your practice
- Name of practitioners including professional qualifications and memberships that you are eligible to include. Check the membership rules for the professional associations that you belong as they all differ.
- Address of your practice, including the post code
- Logo
- Contact details: telephone, fax, email and website
- If you have a limited company, you must include information about this. For example if you bought a company called "Bullion Sales Limited" and you trade as John Smith Associates you would need to include the following wording:

  > *"Bullion Sales Limited trading as John Smith Associates; Registered in England; Company No: ????????; Registered Office: full postal address of registered office."*

- If you are registered for VAT you will need to show the VAT number on your invoices—for simplicity you may also wish to include this in your headed paper. More about VAT in the financial chapters.

These last two points of information can be in very small print but must be somewhere on all your official stationery.

Workbook Design your own stationery:

1.3.6.4 Paper and ink choices:

Paper varies enormously and gives very different messages.

Workbook Design your own stationery:

- *Do you want to use a recycled paper?*

- *Do you want a very distinguished paper such as "Mark of Distinction"?*

- *Do you want a reasonable quality white bond?*

- *Do you want a coloured slightly fancy paper?*

- *If not, what do you want?*

The choice is yours, and the choice you make will determine the look that you create. Make sure that you choose the same paper for everything you do—even the leaflets, as it will look so much more professional.

Choosing a coloured ink will make a big different—black on white is so boring and lacks thought. Talk to other people in case you are colour blind. Make sure that you choose an ink colour that will suit the paper you have chosen and will enhance the message you are giving. If you use shocking pink it will have a very different effect from, say, sepia! When you choose an ink colour, you can use tints of that same colour for no extra cost, using a second ink colour will cost little extra. Think about the whole sheet and the look when you are designing your look. Don't just place the text on the paper. That rarely works.

If you are not sure about your designs, before you commit your money, make sure you are happy. Ask for a proof, this may cost a little, but will be a lot less expensive than printing that you hate. Once you have got a proof show it to some friends and get some feedback.

1.3.7 Your personal image: clothes, rooms, cars

In the same way that your printing gives the impression of your business, so does the way you dress, how you design your consulting room, and the car you drive.

In private business you have a lot more to prove than in the NHS and you will have to work hard—certainly until you have established your reputation. How you dress will be important. Wearing jeans and a T-shirt will give one image; wearing sandals and a long skirt (for the women!) will give another image; wearing a suit will give yet another. There is no right answer about how to dress—this will go hand in hand with your character and what statement you want to give with your appearance.

Example

My first ever supervisor was very fussy about shoes—he said that it said everything about a person's character.

Similar principles will apply to your consulting room:

Workbook Question and Answer Session:

- *Are you trying to give an academic image?*

- *Do you wish to retain a neutral image?*

- *Do you wish the room to feel very homely?*

- *Do you wish the room to look professional?*

- *What other aspects of your image do you need to consider?*

Think about your potential client and what they would expect in answering your questions—not necessarily your personal preferences.

All I have said above applies to cars as well. You may say, the car is not part of your business, but even if you see clients at home and the car is parked in the driveway or sat by the kerb you can be sure your client will notice if you have a Jaguar (client may say "That's where my fees go?" Or "Gosh, this counsellor is doing well!"). An old rust bucket will give a different message.

Whatever you decide about the image you decide to create market test it before you spend too much money on it. By market test I mean ask friends, colleagues and even clients what they think—and listen to the answers.

1.4 Drawing together the threads

Thinking about our two examples, Donna with her group practice, and Simon, with his part-time practice, what would you have suggested each of them did to promote their businesses? You need to think about this realistically, as it is very easy to run away with the costs of advertising and marketing. The budget for advertising and marketing should come to no more than 10% of your income as a rule of thumb. Try also to think, in the case of Donna's practice, where it all went wrong.

CHAPTER TWO

Setting up the structure of the business

"No clients, no business, no money"

2.1 What type of business? The options available to you

Essentially there are four types of businesses:

- Sole trader
- Limited company
- Partnership
- Cooperative

The choice you will make will depend on your personal circumstances and your ambitions. The two options I favour most for the counselling/psychotherapy practitioner are sole trader or limited company. I will therefore discuss them in more detail. Before you decide I would recommend that you discuss your choices with an accountant or business start-up adviser.

A very important piece of advice is to understand that *you are not your business*. Your business needs to be a separate entity to you; think of it as another person if you like. This is very important. It will mean that at some stage you may make decisions that are in the best interest of your business, as opposed to being in your best interest. It is important to understand this and not to confuse the two. It is easier to understand with a limited company as it is a separate legal entity and you will be an employee of the company, which will have its own life blood. You may have an aim to grow the business sufficiently to sell it later on, one very good reason for keeping you and the business separate.

2.1.1 Sole trader

This is how most people begin. This means that you are self-employed. You can be both self-employed and work for someone else at the same time. For example this would be the case if you saw clients in the evening at home but might be working for an employer during the day as is the case with our second example, Simon.

It is very easy to set yourself up as self-employed—all you need to do is to tell your tax inspector or your local Contribution Agency within three months of starting. As they operate a joint registration scheme you only need to tell one office, they will automatically pass the information on to the other office. They will also notify the Customs and Excise office. (I will discuss VAT in a separate section.)

There are fewer formalities for setting up a sole trader. Also, the accountancy requirements are less stringent than for a limited company.

2.1.1.1 The risks involved in being self-employed

The downside of being a sole trader is that you are fully liable if anything goes wrong—the risk of something going wrong is one of the things you need to judge at the outset. For example, if you borrow money, say to buy consulting rooms, and your business fails because you do not get enough clients then you would be personally liable for those debts. In such circumstances you could be made bankrupt or have to sell your house or some other asset to pay the debt. Equally, if you rented consulting rooms and hired a secretary this could make a serious dent on the income you receive from counselling. If you are thinking big, then think long and hard about setting up with a limited company. If your overheads are low and you feel sure (honestly) that your income will be higher than your expenditure then being a sole trader is probably the sensible option for you. It is a question of assessing the risk and during your working career reassessing it from time to time.

I will show in the next section how to budget, set up and maintain accounts as a sole trader.

As a sole trader you will pay Class 2 National Insurance and Class 4 contributions depending on your level of profit. The rate for Class 2 for 2005–06 is £2.10, flat rate, per week plus 8% on profits between £4.895 and £32,760, plus 1% on profits over £32,760. If your earnings are very small you may not have to pay Class 2, but you will have to apply for exemption. It is important that you pay National Insurance contributions as this may otherwise adversely affect your pension forecasts. You can check your pension forecast by contacting the Inland Revenue (see Appendix 1) and asking for a pensions forecast.

As a sole trader you will pay tax on any profits—this will include any personal drawings that you make. You will pay tax on your profits for any one year in three instalments.

2.1.2 Limited company

You can either set up your own limited company (this is not necessary) or buy a company off the shelf. This is what the majority do. Buying a company off the shelf will cost between £80 and £150 plus expenses if you use an accountant or solicitor to complete the formalities.

I *strongly recommend* that if you wish to set up a limited company you ask a solicitor or accountant to help you. Most accountants can do this and you don't really need to involve a solicitor unless there is something complicated about your business or the arrangements between you and any other directors or shareholders. Shop around to find out how much they will charge you for this work as accountant's fee vary enormously (see also section 2.3.4 on choosing an accountant). Getting help will be particularly important if you have other colleagues involved—the best line to take when setting up a business is to sit down and work out all the things that could go wrong and ensure, from the outset, that you put measures in place to prevent these problems occurring.

Setting up a limited company requires quite a lot of form filling—and it is important that these are correctly completed and submitted.

You will also need to have a "registered office"—I recommend you ask your accountant to act as your registered office (especially if you work from home)—some may charge a small fee annually. You will be required to include the company information, including the registered office, on your headed note paper (see section 1.3.6 on designing your headed paper).

If you set up a limited company then you automatically become an employee of the company (even if you own all the shares and are the only director). This means that the company and you pays PAYE tax and Class 1 National Insurance.

For limited companies there is additional tax on company profits—this is known as corporation tax which is currently 19%.

Although the legal, accounting and taxation requirements are more stringent for limited companies, the upside is that as a director of the company you have limited liability—the amount for which you are financially liable is limited to the amount you paid for your shares in the first place. The personal assets of a director can only be touched if the director has acted fraudulently. If you are concerned about your liability you can take out an insurance policy against Directors' Liability.

Limited companies have more credibility with lenders, but unless you are developing a large practice, it is likely that setting up your own practice will require less financial risk than for other kinds of businesses. For the majority of counsellors and psychotherapists this may be an irrelevant point.

If your company has to borrow money, say, to buy or rent premises then the bank may ask you to provide a personal guarantee. You would be liable if you have agreed to provide a personal guarantee—*I strongly urge you NOT to give personal guarantees*—they are so easy to give, and it can cause such heart-ache if things go wrong. People have lost their homes as a result of giving out guarantees too freely.

In addition your accounts have to be set out in a certain way by law for a limited company. You will need to have your accounts filed at the Companies Registration Office. There are penalties if you file your accounts late. If your company sales are more than £5.6 million then you need to have your accounts audited. This will not apply to most of you!

Useful address (England and Wales): Companies Registration Office, Companies House, Crown Way, Cardiff CF4 3UZ; 01222 388 588.

2.1.3 Partnership

This is an extension of being a sole trader in many ways. Although many people do enter into partnerships I strongly advise against it. The biggest reason against this is that all the partners are JOINTLY AND SEVERALLY LIABLE for all the debts in the practice.

For example, if one of your partners runs up a huge business bill, you are personally liable for this, so if the creditor (the person to whom money is owed) cannot get his money from your partner the creditor can come after you for payment. If you do decide on a partnership, then you must have a written partnership agreement between you, drawn up by a solicitor after full discussion of the partnership plans. The solicitor must be experienced in setting up partnerships. Part of that discussion must be what would happen if things go wrong between you. Your accountant may well be able to recommend a suitable solicitor. Remember "there's nowt so queer as folk", and people do change when money is involved.

Think about the partnership that Donna and her colleagues established. Susan's withdrawing from the partnership could make the other partners more financially vulnerable if the partnership agreement is not well constructed for all eventualities.

More recently "limited liability partnerships" have been developed so as to protect the individual from the types of problems highlighted above. Before entering into any type of partnership, limited or otherwise, I would urge you to get good legal advice because everyone's circumstances are different and there is not a "one size fits all" answer to what type of partnership will be right for you.

Useful address: Lawyers for Business Helpline: 0171 405 9075.

2.1.4 Cooperative

The aim of a cooperative is that its workforce must control the management, objectives and use of all assets of a cooperative. Again you will need to consult a solicitor for full details and the type of cooperative most suitable for you. A cooperative, in my opinion, is ideologically very sound and politically correct but may not give you the control of your business that you may be looking for.

Useful address: ICOM, Vassalli House, 20 Central Road, Leeds LS1 6DE; 0161 246 2959.

Workbook Question and Answer Session:

- *What are the financial risks involved in the project you are planning?*

- *Are you in charge of these risks or are there other parties involved in the decision-making and control of the project?*

- *Which type of legal/business structure would best protect you and your proposed practice and the risks involved?*

Donna's example

Going back to our case study of Donna in the introduction, what could she and her colleagues have done differently that would have protected each of them in a far more robust way than the partnership they put together?

And why?

2.2 Setting up and maintaining your accounts

You cannot be good at everything and if accounts are difficult for you then, it's quite simple, get a book-keeper. A good book-keeper is worth their salt, and should save you money in the long term, and will certainly save your sanity. Book-keepers are not easy to find—the best way is to ask around. Usually a book-keeper will just need to do a couple of hours a month to keep your accounts up-to-date.

Workbook Question and Answer Session:

On a scale of 1–10 (10 being the best) how good am I at understanding and keeping accounts?

If your answer is less than 7 you need to think either of
- *getting some training (if you think it would make any difference), or*
- *hiring a book-keeper.*

Would I be better off getting some simple book-keeping training or a book-keeper? (remember the time implication)

2.2.1 Accounting for a sole trader

The accounts for a sole trader are very straightforward. You will need to demonstrate to the Inland Revenue proof of all your expenditure and income. You can maintain your accounts manually or on a computer. (At the very worst, put all your receipts in a shoe-box and take them to the accountant—but this is an expensive way of doing your accounts!)

At the outset you should decide how you are going to keep your accounts and implement a system and decide on a financial year-end. People quite often make this 5th April to tie in with the tax year.

If the amount of income per financial year is less than £15,000 then all you will need to do is to work out your income and expenditure and your profit or loss and insert these figures in your tax return. Over and above this figure you will need to provide formal accounts.

2.2.2 Accounting for a limited company

If you are setting up a limited company it is essential that you take the advice of an accountant BEFORE setting up your accounts because every accountant has their preferred style and preferred accounting package. You may need to take legal advice, especially if there are several of you joining together.

2.2.3 Choosing your accounting system: the different formats available for doing your accounts

2.2.3.1 Computerised accountancy package

If you are computer literate then you may prefer to work with a dedicated accountancy program. There are a number on the market—but they are NOT for the faint hearted—if you view accounts as a worry please give this option a miss—and get a book-keeper! If you opt to have a limited company your accountant is most likely to want you to keep your accounts on a reputable dedicated accountancy software such as Sage.

2.2.3.2 Spreadsheet

Equally if you are computer literate then setting up your accounts on a spreadsheet will save you a lot of trouble (for example, no adding up manually!). What you need to include on a spreadsheet will be the same as for a manual system so I shall discuss the style of record keeping later in this section. This type of book-keeping is fine for a sole trader, but if you are opting for a limited company then discuss this with your accountant before you start working on your accounts.

2.2.3.3 *Manual accounts*

For a counsellor keeping manual accounts is quite a possibility as counselling business accounts are pretty straightforward. You can buy a book in which to record your accounts, called a cash book), from good stationers—for example the Cathedral series. Buy one with about 30 columns. Working in pencil is not a bad idea as it is easy to correct!!

See the section on record keeping in the next section to see what to include in your accounts.

Workbook Question and Answer Session:

What sort of accounting system would suit my business best (regardless of whether I or a book-keeper do the work)?

- *Accountancy package*

- *Spreadsheet*

- *Manual book-keeping*

2.3 Office practicalities

2.3.1 Record keeping

Once you have chosen how to keep your accounts you will need to set up how you intend to maintain them. See Appendix 3 for an example of what you may want to include. Please remember, everyone sets up their business in different ways so you will have to fiddle with it to make it work for you. If you can manage to keep your accounts up-to-date to this level then you will save yourself a fortune on accountancy fees.

2.3.2 Billing your clients

Buy yourself a duplicate invoicing book to record ALL your income.

Always, but always, give an invoice/receipt (not quite the same thing) for work. Do not allow yourself to slip money in your pocket without accounting for it—the Inland Revenue will never leave you alone again if you are caught doing that, it simply is not worth it.

The difference between an invoice and a receipt is very simple: you give a receipt for money received (technically known as cash sales), and an invoice if you will receive the money at a later date (technically known as debtors).

The issue of money is always tricky in counselling and psycho-therapy. At first you may feel awkward about this, but you must be firm. Otherwise, it will be just one of the ways in which your clients may test you. You need to set up a system for dealing with the money that you are comfortable with—in reality what you are doing from a business point of view is selling your time and expertise in 50-minute slots. These slots are no different than if you go to a solicitor—he will bill you in time slots and, taking the idea further, are no different than say selling car components. This is the point where you have to be very firm with yourself and remind yourself that you are running a business not a charity.

My practice is to bill in advance. This way, you will not have to chase debts (one of the biggest sources of time-wasting in a business). Your clients are far more likely to be reliable if they have paid up front. Remember the old adage—"*old debt is difficult to collect*".

I usually see the client the first time for a one-off 50 minute session, with no strings attached on either side. The client pays in the usual way. I normally spend 5–10 minutes towards the end of the session discussing how the client felt about the session and whether they would feel comfortable continuing.

Workbook Question and Answer Session:

How am I going to collect the money?

What forms of payment will I accept?

How am I going to record this and give a receipt?

2.3.3 Terms and Conditions

If the client wants to continue then I go through my Terms and Conditions. You may wish to give your client a written list of these. You may prefer to have them printed up on the wall. You may wish to include the Terms and Conditions in a more general Information Sheet about yourself and your practice (see sections 4.1 and 4.12). The main Terms and Conditions that you may wish to consider are:

How you bill   I usually book appointments for 4 or 6 weeks at a stretch for which the client pays upfront. The idea of the time scale is both that it is manageable financially for the client, and it is a useful period of time after which I always review progress with the client, obviously depending on your chosen method of working.

How you collect the money   Your clients will want to pay you in a variety of ways. The most important thing is *to get your payment as quickly as possible*. You may wish to accept payment by cash, cheque and credit card (you can do this easily and cheaply enough through PayPal).

Cancellations   I always insist on 24 hours' notice for a cancellation. If the client cancels with less than 24 hours' notice then they lose money for the session. With more than 24 hours I will rearrange appointments. If a client keeps changing appointments then I review this with the client, though in practice it rarely happens if they have paid upfront.

Time keeping   I am very strict about time-keeping, though occasionally there will be emergencies of one sort or another. If you let this slip through kindness you will make a rod for your own back—I am sure that such issues will have been covered in your training course.

Safety   Counselling and psychotherapy are unpredictable professions where issues of danger and safety need to be thought about (I will cover this elsewhere as well). You should let your client know at the outset what is unacceptable behaviour within the sessions.

Contact between sessions   Your clients may be at an acute stage of crisis where some support is necessary between sessions. You should decide what you are happy to accept in the way of contact and let the client know. You may not wish to raise this subject unless it looks like becoming an issue. Clients may also need to change appointments—it is helpful for them to have a clear time at which they can ring.

Your own illness/death Whatever policy you develop for informing clients of your own illness or death, it is a useful item to include in your Terms and Conditions. This way your client will not be surprised or alarmed if someone else calls you in event of an emergency.

Workbook Question and Answer Session:

How am I going to set the parameters of the counselling?

How am I going to provide the client with the Terms and Conditions?

What are my Terms and Conditions going to include?

2.3.4 Choosing your accountant

Choosing your accountant is one of the most important decisions you will make in the setting up of your business. There are a number of criteria to think about:

- You must like and be able to get on with your accountant.
- You must be able to understand what he is talking about—if you can't, move on.
- You must have confidence in him/her—if not, move on.
- He/she must understand the specifics of running a counselling business (as opposed to any other) and the specific issues that arise—such as around confidentiality.
- You should discuss how much he will charge and how those charges will be made up. Get this in writing.
- You should discuss when and how you will be billed—ask for a full breakdown on your invoice.
- He should be able to advise you on how to set out your accounts, how to budget.
- He should advise you as to the best year ending for you. Most of us have our financial year ending to coincide with the tax year in April.
- Check the accountants qualifications.

Most accountants will give you an initial free session in which you can discuss the above. If you are not entirely at peace about your accountant shop around until you find one that you feel comfortable with. Ask your colleagues, they may well be able to recommend someone locally that they use. Remember London prices are generally more expensive. You will find details of chartered accountants in Appendix 1.

Workbook Question and Answer Session:

Who is going to be my accountant?

Why am I choosing this person/company?

2.4 Business planning

"Everyone told me I should do a business plan and how valuable it was, and, of course, I thought I knew better and ignored the advice." How often do we hear this sort of comment!?

The trouble is it is very tedious doing this and words like profit and loss and cash flow forecast are designed to send some of us to an early grave. But if you are going to run a business you MUST do this.

The best advice I can give you is this: go round the banks where you live (this will take some time and may involve appointments) and ask to see the Small Business Manager.

Banks are marvellous and terrible—remember they are a business just like everyone else and if they think their money is at risk they'll want to minimise their risk.

All banks are after your business so you will be looked after very well for the first 12–18 months, including getting free banking during this period. I will talk more about banking itself later, but the benefit of doing the rounds of the banks is that they distribute excellent starter packs for small businesses. This includes charts to complete your business plan, profit and loss and cash flow forecasts.

These packs are fairly idiot-proof and I do recommend them. Choose the one that you feel most comfortable with, regardless of whether you are going to open an account with their bank. The advantage of following through with one of these packs is that it will make you think about all sorts of things that you had probably never thought about.

If you are in a position where you need some start-up capital do not even think of approaching anyone or any organisation without having completed your three start-up items:

- the business plan
- the profit and loss
- the cash flow forecast

In the sections below I shall cover these in more detail so please do not worry if you don't know what these items are. In Section 2.4 you will find a skeleton for creating a business plan. In Appendix 2 you will find examples of a profit and loss and a cash flow forecast.

2.4.1 The business plan

The secret of a business plan is to keep it short—for a small counselling business not more than two sides of paper plus appendices with profit and loss and cash flow forecasts. It is something that you will wish to review periodically. It should be comprehensible to the bank manager, accountant, solicitor and anyone who may need to lend you money. After reading it the reader should have a clear understanding of what counselling/psychotherapy is and what type of service you intend to provide.

There are two main reasons for writing a business plan:
1   To focus your thinking and concretise your plans. It will make a useful document for you to review at later stages to see how your business has progressed.
2.   As the basis for a request for borrowing.

What to include:
I   A brief, easy-to-understand description of counselling
II   A brief summary of the business you are planning:

    (a) *Practicalities:*   Location

                                   Management and staffing of the business

                                   Type of business structure (e.g. sole trader, limited company)

    (b) *Marketing:*   Your client "profile"

                                   Your target client group

                                   Your competitors

                                   How you will get your clients

(c) *Development:*   The potential for the business

(d) *Financial forecasts:*   Profit and Loss forecast for two years, on a monthly basis

Cash Flow forecast for two years, on a monthly basis

Any borrowing requirements—fully explained

(e) *Prospects:*   What you intend to achieve by a certain date

Risk analysis (e.g. Are you fully dependent on the business or will you have other income?)

(f) *About you:*   Personal information about you and any colleagues who will be working with you—a short CV of relevant information, including:

- any previous experience of running a business
- counselling experience
- achievements—you do not need to include a complete record of your work history

---

Workbook Question and Answer Session:

What to include:

1 A brief, easy-to-understand description of counselling

II A brief summary of the business you are planning:

   (a) *Practicalities:*   Location

                           Management and staffing of the business

                           Business structure

   (b) *Marketing:*   Your client "profile"

                           Your target client group

                           Your competitors

                           How you will get your clients

(c) *Development:*   The potential for the business

(d) *Financial forecasts:*
- Profit and Loss forecast for two years

- Cash Flow forecast for two years

(e) *Prospects:*
- What you intend to achieve (give timetable):

- Risk analysis

(f) *About you:*   *Personal relevant information about you and any colleagues*

2.4.2 Profit and Loss and Cash Flow forecasts

Profit and Loss forecasts show when the transactions take place.

Cash Flow forecasts show when the money actually changes hands. Not handling the cash flow correctly or having an inadequate cash flow is the single biggest cause for the failure of a business. As counsellors we are very poor at asking for money. To make your business a success you will need to become quite hardened to asking for the money, and preferably upfront.

Example

In your profit and loss you forecast that in May you will receive £600 in income from counselling fees. Your monthly outgoings for the month of May (i.e. when you will pay them, not when they were invoiced) are £540. Theoretically you should have £60 profit. BUT, client X deliberately forgot his cheque book and you did not get paid the £150 he owed you and you did not see him again until June. At the end of May you will therefore in reality in debt by £90, even though you know the money will come in when you next see your client. This may mean the difference between being able to pay your monthly rent, or not.

Solution: You may be able to accept credit card payments through PayPal. You need to be firm with your client.

Cash flow is therefore KING, the profit and loss merely tells us what we are going to earn and spend and when those invoices will be raised.

If things are a bit tight you can help your cash flow by either getting the money in sooner, or delaying some payments (not to be encouraged as you will get a bad name if you do this too often).

Many people (including those in business) are sceptical about forecasting. They say, "Well how do I know how much electricity I will use, or how many clients I will have—it is like putting your finger in the air and feeling for the wind".

There is some truth in this, but planning will give you a base line to work to. My rule of thumb is to be pessimistic about income and expenditure. A profit and loss can be very detailed, or you can do it on the back of an envelope. Sometimes the expenses are divided into direct costs (e.g. the cost of beer if you were running a pub) and indirect costs (e.g. general staffing costs that cannot be attributed to a particular sale). For you, setting up at the beginning I suggest you either use one of the bank forms, or develop your own system from one of them to make sure you haven't forgotten any expenditure.

There are many costs that you as a counsellor can include that you may not have thought about. Get into the habit of *always* asking for a receipt for your accounts, as you will need proof of your expenditure. For example, if you work from home you can claim a proportion of your utility bills. If you are doing a course, you can include the course fees. You can include your personal therapy, any books that you use for study, and travelling expenses. If you use your car in the course of your work (as opposed to travelling to work) then you can claim a proportion of the costs (you need to check the rules for this with your accountant as the Inland Revenue has very strict rules for this, and the rules are different between a sole trader and a limited company). Don't worry about proportions at this stage, that is where the accountant comes in useful, as he will know the latest regulations and allowances.

You will need to give as much information as possible in the Profit and Loss forecast, and try to allocate the expenditure to the month as carefully as possible. The miscellaneous column should be empty!

For a *Profit and Loss* forecast you allocate the expenditure at the point *where you order or use the goods, or the invoice was raised by the supplier*, regardless of when you pay for them.

Profit and Loss Example for EXPENDITURE

The telephone bill comes every 2–3 months (depending on your telephone company and type of account). But you will use the telephone every month. So allocate some expenditure each month even though the cash flow will show you will not pay it until July. You allocate this to the May, June and July Profit and Loss forecast, and the July Cash Flow budget, as this is when you would pay the money out of your account.

EXPENDITURE Profit and Loss forecast:

Expenditure	May	June	July
Telephone	−£50	−£50	−£50

EXPENDITURE Cash Flow forecast:

Payments	May	June	July
Telephone			£150

Profit and Loss Example for INCOME

On the income side you will allocate the amount of counselling sessions times the cost of the session per month, regardless of when you receive the money. For example, if in June you antici-pated eight counselling sessions at £30 then you would allocate £240 to the June Profit and Loss budget. If you thought that you would receive £200 of this money in June and £40 of this money in July then allocate £200 to the June Cash Flow account and £40 to the July Cash Flow.

INCOME Profit and Loss:

Sales (Note 1)	*June*	*July*
Clients @ £35.00 per hour	240	

INCOME Cash Flow:

Receipts (Note 1)	*June*	*July*
Clients @ £35.00 per hour	200	40

What I am attempting to demonstrate is that getting your money in promptly is very important. When making your forecasts I suggest that you are pessimistic about the amount of income you will receive and over budget for the expenditure you will make. This way you are least likely to get things wrong.

In your first year of business you may not get your forecasts correct, but gradually you will come to see the peaks and troughs of business and then you will be able to forecast more accurately. Doing these types of forecasts can help to tell you when it is not worth working—for example you may find by tracking these figures that each year you have a dip in August—perhaps that tells you that this is the best time for you also to take a holiday. Or, it is the time to do the accounts and other office administration without interruption—I love working in August as you can get so much done.

In an ideal world you should do your accounts monthly and have columns on both your Profit and Loss forecast and your Cash Flow forecast for both *anticipated* and *actual* income and expenditure. This way you can see how well you are doing, or, in the case of a shortfall, you can pinpoint a cash flow problem and take remedial action.

See Appendix 2 at the back of the book for an example of Profit and Loss and Cash Flow forecasts. Please note that the end figure should look the same for both forecasts as it is just a different way of arriving at the same figures.

Workbook Question and Answer Session:

Have I prepared a Profit and Loss forecast? If not, why not?

Have I prepared a Cash Flow forecast? If not, why not?

If you are not going to prepare these documents you will need to have a cast iron reason not to!

2.4.3 Banking

Banks can be wonderful, and they can be terrible. The most important thing to remember is that no matter how friendly they are and how much they woo you for your business, the bank is a business like all others, and in the long run it will make its money from you and will turn its back on you just when you need help the most.

That said, all the high street banks now operate special departments for small businesses, produce excellent packages for those starting up in business and will give you a lot of help and advice free of charge. You will get between 12 and 18 months free banking for a new business. The additional 6 months may well be dependent on you attending a local business course—the bank will see this as an investment in its money as your business is less likely to go wrong if you have received some advice and training on small businesses. As a practising counsellor I am happy to put my head on the block and say that our skills are more on the people front. Few of us have experience in the running of a business, so these courses are brilliant—and usually at convenient times—such as at the weekend.

In my humble opinion the most important ingredient is your relationship with the official of the bank that you will deal with. Whilst you must always watch your bank charges and negotiate over them, having a bank manager that you get on with far outweighs paying a little more for the account—and being able to get hold of their direct line telephone number!

Workbook Question and Answer Session:

Have I prepared the Profit and Loss and Cash Flow forecasts? If not why not?

Have I fully researched all the banking options?

Do I want a high street bank with a manager?

Do I want an internet or telephone bank (remote but cheaper)?

2.4.4 Profit

It is quite likely that you may not need to borrow any or a great deal to get your business going as counselling is a service industry and needs investment, other than your training, to start up.

Whatever your start-point you should always aim to make a profit—otherwise, why are you in business?

It is very important that you separate the caring part of yourself from your business—mixing one with the other will have disastrous consequences. *Your primary aim as a business is to make money.*

The Inland Revenue will question your accounts if you regularly make a loss and will wish to investigate you. If, when you do your forecasts, you cannot foresee a profit then you need to ask yourself some serious questions about whether the business is appropriate and viable.

Workbook Question and Answer Session:

Have I been brutal with myself and seen that unless I view my hours as sales items I will not make a profit?

If not, why do I still think I can make a go of running a business?

2.4.5 What you can charge

This is like asking "How long is a piece of string?" The answer has to be a combination. You will need to consider:

- Your client group (by changing client group you could increase or decrease your income quite dramatically)
- What your client group can afford

- What you need to earn to break even versus how many hours you need to work (don't forget to allow for paying tax)
- What your qualifications are
- The geographical/social locality.

The way to work out whether it all adds up to profit is to design your profit and loss sheet, working out the expenditure first. Then play with the income to see how that works over a year. You will need to remember that clients take holidays, need gaps for other reasons or may leave. You need to include seasonal adjustments.

The bottom line is if your figures do not stack up you should be having second thoughts about running a private practice, a business, as you may have a high chance of failure.

Workbook Question and Answer Session:

In this section you will look at the maximum and the minimum you can earn, then you will need to decide what is reasonable, using other criteria, such as what is ethical and manageable.

How am I going to set my pricing structure?

What is the maximum I could earn?

Working out 1

Your maximum hours available	*What you will charge*	*The weekly total*
	£	£ per week

Working out 2

The ideal hours available	What you will charge	The weekly total
	£	£ per week

Working out 3

Your minimum hours available	What you will charge	The weekly total
	£	£ per week

Based on these figures and my own personal ability and capability to work, how many hours is it reasonable for me to work?

Based on this number of hours and the amount you will charge what is your intended weekly income that you will aim for?

Number of hours you can work	What you will charge	The weekly total you will earn
	£	£ per week

2.4.6 Going bust

Please do not skip this section! Every business has the ability for success and failure. We hope you will be successful and doing careful business planning and monitoring your business plan and financial forecasts against the reality is very important. However, sometimes, for reasons that may or may not have anything to do with you, your business may fail.

Ideally, if you are keeping a careful eye on everything then you can make decisions early. For example, Donna and her team should have been far shrewder about their initial plans and tracked everything. If they had done this earlier then, they would have worked out within two months that the business they had planned was not going to work in the way they envisaged. They still would not have lost too much money and could have changed course with positive effects. They did not have the necessary business experience to see that and would probably have benefited from the skills of either some business coaching or a part-time business manager.

If you do get into trouble financially, then taking early action will save you time, money and your reputation.

2.4.7 Risk taking

As part of your planning you will need to look at the risks associated with your business. You will need to take some risks, but you will need to be very clear about the level of risk you are entering into. For example, borrowing £25,000 against your house for the business is a medium risk, but borrowing £250,000 may be a financially suicidal risk.

As a woman working in isolation, you will need to be careful about the clients you select.

There are risks on both the business and professional sides. Use the boxes overleaf to help you identify the risks associated.

Professional Counselling and Psychotherapy RISKS	Risks you can afford to take
	Risks you mustn't take
Business RISKS	Risks you can afford to take
	Risks you mustn't take

2.5 Drawing together the threads

Thinking about our two examples, Donna with her group practice, and Simon, with his part-time practice, did they choose the right business structure?

- When things went wrong for Donna's partnership, how could they have used their book-keeping and accountancy to inform them of their progress, or lack of it.
- Should they have tracked this against their business plan?
- Should they have bought in, or brought in, specialist managerial help?
- Did they allocate responsibilities for different areas of the business? Would this have helped?
- What similarity is there between either Donna's or Simon's examples and your own business plans?
- What have you learned about how not to do it?!

CHAPTER THREE

The practicalities of running the business

3.1 Financial aspects

3.1.1 Book-keeping

I have written quite a lot already about setting up your accounts. If you are like me you will throw everything in a filing tray with the intention of updating the accounts tomorrow, but as we all know, tomorrow never comes!

If you are in this category, to avoid falling into this trap, I would like to make a suggestion that will save you a lot of grief, and not cost too much: get a book-keeper.

Advantages

Using the services of a book-keeper is tax-deductible.

You will be freer to concentrate on what you are good at: counselling.

Your accounts will always be up-to-date and you will know how well you are doing.

How will I find a book-keeper?   You can ask your accountant or your local colleagues if they know of someone, or even look in Yellow Pages. (Look under Book-keeping Services or Accountancy Services.) You will probably only need someone for a couple of hours a month. This is the best money I have spent in my business and will free you of endless anxieties of tax returns, VAT returns, double-entry booking, computerised accounts and the other horrors that accountants manage to think of. I wish I had done this years ago: for many years I did my own books—misguidedly thinking I would be saving money. Using the services of a book-keeper is an allowable business expense and frees you to concentrate on what you are good at: the people business.

3.1.2 Pensions

You should receive a state pension, provided you have paid sufficient contributions, but that won't keep you in coffee beans. You will probably want to create an additional pension. Depending on the status of your business you can set up different types of pensions.

What is absolutely sure is that creating a pension is a tax efficient way of saving—most of us do not invest enough into our pensions and do not start to do so early enough. I am not going to go into more detail than that as pensions are complicated and whatever I say will be out-of-date before the ink has dried. Also everyone's circumstances are so unique that blanket advice cannot be given.

My advice on this front is to make contact with a financial adviser. The biggest problem is to find one whom you can really trust and be sure that they are selling you the right product for your needs.

There are essentially two kinds of financial adviser: **tied** (to one company) and **independent**.

The disadvantage of a tied adviser is that they can only sell the product range from their company. However, if you do your homework and know the market standing of the company (such as one of the top five) then a financial adviser from one of these companies may be extremely good. Ask to see evidence of their performance. Remember every company will present its performance in the best light possible. You could look at Which? Magazine for more a objective view.

Independent advisers can theoretically sell you a much wider range of products from different companies—they will all have their pet favourites, and may be on preferential commission from certain companies. I sometimes wonder how "independent" they really are. You can ask them what commission they will receive.

If you find yourself a good financial adviser he/she should be able to advise you on all aspects of your insurance needs—even if he/she can't provide every area. If you use an independent financial adviser make sure he/she is registered with the Financial Services Authority for the area of work he/she is advising you on.

As an employer, if you have more than five employees you have to offer to administer a Stakeholder Pension Scheme.

3.1.3 Payroll

Sole trader   As a sole trader you can take drawings out of your business as and when you want. These will be listed within your accounts and you will be taxed on them when the payments become due for that financial year. In practice this means there can be a long delay between when you earn the money and when the tax becomes due. There is therefore a danger of spending it?

Advice: decide with your accountant what your potential tax liability might be, work out a monthly sum to set aside and put this in a deposit account and DO NOT TOUCH IT!

If you employ any staff you will be required to deduct income tax and National Insurance via the PAYE scheme.

Limited company   As a director you will be an employee of the company, you and any staff that you employ must be paid net of any tax and National Insurance under the PAYE scheme. There are ways round this such as taking dividends. Before taking these decisions you need to talk to a qualified person who is aware of all your personal and business circumstances as each decision will have longer-term ramifications.

You can operate the PAYE scheme yourself, but for a very small amount you can use the services of your book-keeper, accountant or a payroll company (see Payroll Services in Yellow Pages). There is so much red tape that I thoroughly recommend this. Each month they will supply you with all the documentation and pay slips.

All you will need to do each month, once you have this information is to complete the PAYE docket (in the yellow Inland Revenue paying-in docket book that you will receive when you apply to set up the PAYE scheme for your business). Calculate from the information you have the total amount due and send the docket and a cheque for that amount to the Inland Revenue.

Do not allow yourself to fall behind with these payments as they can mount up very quickly. The Inland Revenue is very keen on reminders in any case.

Don't forget what I said earlier about a limited company being a separate entity to yourself.

3.1.4 Tax and NI

I have already explained the different taxation systems according to your type of business.

Sole traders   If you are self-employed then you will pay tax twice a year. The biggest danger is not saving for this. As I have already mentioned above, I thoroughly recommend that you open a second high-interest bank account into which you pay approximately 20% of your income. (More, if your income is in the higher rate band (40%).) You should not have to pay this much as you will be able to deduct business expenses, but this way you will be sure to cover yourself. You will also need to pay a weekly National Insurance contribution.

Limited company Tax and NI are organised via the PAYE scheme. When you set up the company you will fill in a form to set this up. You will receive a booklet with a number of monthly dockets. Dividends are often the most tax-effective way to pay yourself as long as the business is profitable. You will need to discuss with your accountant the pro's and con's of how to pay yourself.

3.1.5 Insurance

There are a number of different types of insurance that you may wish to consider. You can spend a fortune on insurance so you will have to weigh up the merits of some types of insurance before deciding whether to insure yourself.

There are two insurances that are mandatory: **employers' and public liability**.

3.1.5.1 Business insurance

You can get a whole package that usually includes the items listed below (and more). All the banks offer business insurance. You may wish to join the Federation of Small Businesses as they offer a very good scheme (it is also very useful for contacts and advice).

3.1.5.1.A Mandatory insurances

Employers' liability At the very minimum you must have employers' liability insurance. This should be for at least £2,000,000. The law also requires you to display a certificate of employers' liability insurance in the work place.

Public liability   This covers your liability for any visitors and clients to your premises. For example if someone tripped over a cable.

Workbook Question and Answer Session:

Have I purchased public liability and employer liability insurance?

Have I put up the Certificate in the office?

What other business insurance do I need? (Read on below and then come back and complete this section.)

How much extra will these additional items cost?

On a scale of 1–10 how much do I need each of them?

You are the only person who can judge what insurance you need— remember that you need to balance the cost with the potential protection.

3.1.5.1.B Desirable insurances

Fire & damage   This covers destruction or damage to property and is a good idea if you have premises and equipment. You can also insure against loss of profits in the event of a fire or other insured peril. If you can easily relocate consulting rooms/office then this insurance may not be as essential.

Theft   Forced entry and/or exit from your work place. If you want to be covered against theft by your employees or visitors, you will need to pay extra and get fidelity insurance.

Working from home   If you work from home, don't forget to tell your home insurers otherwise you may find that you are not covered. You may need to pay an additional premium.

Loss of money   Cash and cheques can be insured against theft from the work place, in transit to the bank etc.

Computer records   You should think about this especially within the context of your clients' records, the changing law surrounding this, the Code of Ethics that you adhere to and current legislation including the Data Protection Act 1998 which requires you to obtain a client's consent for records to be kept. As I understand things at the moment you would not be wise to keep client records on the computer. You may wish to maintain them in a computerised form, but I recommend you store the records on a CD/floppy disk in a locked fire-proof cabinet.

Business machines and equipment   You may wish to consider this—and it depends what is included in the theft section of your insurance. Always read the small print.

Professional liability/Professional indemnity   As a practising counsellor you *would be crazy* not to have this insurance. This covers you against claims by your clients for damages caused through your negligence or misconduct. Never be tempted to underinsure. You should contact your professional body for details of recommended speciality insurers.

This product is very specialised for counsellors. Be careful to make sure that you choose a scheme that knows about the specific requirements of counselling and psychotherapy.

Director's liability   If you run a limited company that protects you against claims of fraud and incompetence.

3.1.5.2 Health insurances

Keyman   If your business is very dependent on you or one of your colleagues (for example you can't easily send in a substitute for a counselling session, unlike if you were servicing a car) you may wish to consider this insurance. Keyman insurance will pay out, for example, £250,000 if you die. To get this cover you have to be able to prove that the person's death would cost the business money.

Private health   Although this is quite expensive the advantage is that, if you do have to have an operation, you can have it at your convenience, not at the NHS's whim. This means you can plan your absence for least inconvenience to yourself and your clients. There are some ways to keep the cost of this insurance down, by for example having a policy that kicks in only if you cannot get the required health care within the NHS within a specific time frame, for example 6 weeks.

Permanent health   This pays out an income if you became too ill to work. The disadvantage of this is that it is quite expensive. If you are young (say around 30) the policy may not be too expensive and the advantage is that it does not increase in cost over the years.

To summarise, there are numerous other business protection policies. You will need to evaluate their appropriateness for you versus their cost.

Workbook Question and Answer Session:

What policies MUST I have?

What will the annual cost of all these policies be?

What policies would I like?

What will the annual cost of all these policies be?

3.1.6 VAT

The first criterion to consider is your anticipated income. If your income in any twelve months will come to more than £60,000 then you will have no choice, you will have to become VAT registered.

If you do have the choice in the matter, given that counselling is a service industry it is unlikely to be in your interest to become VAT registered. In other words you don't buy in raw materials, make your product and then sell it on at a profit. You just sell your hours.

I am going to show two examples to demonstrate what I mean, using the same sums of money for the sales (income) side of the equation to show the effect and cost of VAT to you

Example 1—The purchase and sale of items where VAT is attached to both the sale and the purchase—using the example of buying and selling bricks

	Cost (ex. VAT)	VAT (17.5%)	Cost (inc VAT)
You will pay VAT on the materials you buy	£3,500.00	£612.50	£4,112.50
You will charge VAT on the sale price	£4,365.00	£763.88	£5,128.88
Profit	£865	£151.38	£1,016.38
You will pay VAT on the profit		**£151.38**	

Example 2—where you largely sell your hours—for example selling counselling hours

	Cost (ex. VAT)	VAT (17.5%)	Cost (inc VAT)
You will pay VAT on the materials you buy e.g. stationery	£700.00	£122.50	£822.50
You will charge VAT on the sale price, your counselling hours	£4,365.00	£763.88	£5,128.88
Profit	£3,665.00	£641.38	£4306.38
You will pay VAT on the profit		£641.38	

You will see in example 2, the one most likely to be relevant to you that you pay more VAT, because you have less costs to set against the income. This demonstrates that, on the whole, I would not recommend being VAT registered if you have a choice, as you will not benefit as a service industry and all you are doing is doing the government's job—collecting their tax at your expense and effort.

Every three months you will complete a VAT quarterly return. You will list the sum of the VAT you paid on your purchases, and you will list the sum of the VAT that you charged on your sales. It is likely that you will have charged more VAT that you will have paid so you will need to subtract the sales from the purchases to get the difference. That is what you send to Customs and Excise.

There is also a Flat Rate Scheme, where you simply pay a fixed percentage of your sales as VAT and you do not have to claim back VAT on your input costs.

If you are unsure about the best method for you, you should take advice from an accountant.

We call counselling a service industry, because you are providing a service. You will buy a few things, but very little, and you would have to charge VAT on all your counselling sessions. This either means that your clients would have to pay 17.5% more for each session, and very few of them would be able to reclaim the VAT, or you get 17.5% less income—neither is desirable if it is avoidable. Also you would need to ensure that you save your VAT as you need to pay this at the end of each quarter—the same advice applies as for income tax—work out what you are likely to be paying out for each VAT return and put this sum aside each week.

My overall advice to you is that unless you have to, you would probably do better not to be VAT registered. But again, please talk to your accountant about your personal circumstances before making any decision.

Useful website: HM Revenue and Customs
http://www. hmrc.gov.uk

3.2 Staffing and personnel issues

3.2.1 Getting staff

Hiring, retaining and dismissing staff is really quite difficult. You have a number of options for getting your staff:

- Employment agencies
- Adverts in local newspapers
- Word of mouth

Wherever you advertise—I suggest you keep the advert very general in the first instance, as any mention of a counselling or psychotherapy practice may bring out the do-gooders, the cranks or those in need of counselling themselves.

You may wish them to submit a CV and a short statement about themselves and why they think they are suitable for the post. The short statement shows much more than the CV, which will be well worked and may disguise short-comings. It is very common to ask people to fill in an application form as it involves much more effort than merely sending a CV.

If you are beginning a new business and you are not sure whether you can afford another salary you may wish to consider taking on a younger person (and sometimes a not so young person returning to work) from one of the schemes, such as New Deal or Modern Apprenticeship. The Job Centre with give you the New Deal details and your local Careers Office will give you apprenticeship details. If you do take on a trainee you must be prepared to train them and give them sufficient time to develop their confidence and skills. I have taken a member of staff via this route and it has been very successful. Their salaries are subsidised for a period of time and you can also get financial help with their training.

Whatever route you take to getting a member of staff you may have to have several attempts before you get the right person.

3.2.2 Job description

Before setting out to advertise for staff put together a job description. This should include the following:

- The job title
- A brief description of the duties
- Skills required
- Responsibilities
- Career prospects
- To whom the employee is answerable
- Hours of work and holidays
- Salary scale and any pension details
- Future training

3.2.3 Choosing your staff

The biggest issue in your choice of staff will be their ability to keep confidentiality and to field calls from distressed people. You will also have to consider the usual issues of honesty, suitability, skills, common sense and initiative. You may wish them to undergo a health check.

You will need to short-list any applications for the job. Do not tell anyone that they have not got the job until your new employee confirms in writing that they accept the position and you have checked their references.

You will wish to interview potentially suitable candidates. This gives both you and the interviewee the opportunity to assess each other.

When making your short list you will need to try and match your ideal list of skills most closely with the applications. Even then when you interview candidates you may find that you choose someone who has less skills on your list but with whom you think you could develop a good working relationship.

Before you interview, draw up a list of questions to ask and essential information that you will give each interviewee. Much of the essential will derive from the job description. The question you ask should be quite searching, I'm sure your counselling skills will help here! More than the answers you are given, look out for what you are not told.

When interviewing you should try to ask each of the candidates the same questions and give them the same information. This is necessary so as not to discriminate. Thinking about where you will interview and who will make up the interview panel. It can be useful to have an additional person present, even if you ask a colleague to sit in to give you a second opinion.

Before you engage any staff always give them a skills test. For example if you want them to use a computer, don't just take their word that they can use a computer, get them to compose a letter. You will be amazed at how many people cannot correctly set out a letter or spell. Ask them to answer the phone, and get someone to phone in being a rather difficult client. See how they react.

When you have interviewed everyone, go through the candidates listing the pros and cons. If you can choose someone then take up references. It is better to speak to a referee, you can get a better sense of the truth. Ask the referees some searching questions.

When you offer the job you should confirm this in writing, and make the offer confidential upon satisfactory references and medical (if you think this is necessary). This letter (and the ad) forms part of an employee's contact of employment. You will probably want to include a probationary period of 3–6 months.

3.2.4 Legal requirements as an employer

These are quite complicated and vary with the length of time the employee has been with you. You can get useful booklets giving guidance on employment from the DTI.

- You must not discriminate because of sex, marital status, age or race in ads, interviews and job descriptions.
- You must tell your tax office when you take on a new employee.
- You must give your employee a contract of employment and letter of appointment. It is also useful to include your Grievance Policy and Disciplinary Procedure. This must be done within two months of starting work. You can buy packs that

include templates of contracts, business letters, etc. By using such a package you can be more sure that what you say in your letter of engagement or contract will be legally accurate and up-to-date.

Useful address: DTI Publications Orderline, Admail 528, London SW1W 8YT; 0870 150 2500.

Useful software with templates: PlanIt Business Suite—including contracts and agreements, legal letters, staff appraiser, health and safety, business plan and general letters. PlanIt Software Ltd., 75 Wadham Road, London SW15 2YR. You can buy this package on line and download it at www.**planit**.co.uk/**planit**Catalog/index.php.

3.2.5 Record keeping and confidentiality

In addition to the usual business confidentiality your staff should complete a confidentiality agreement (sample in Appendix 4). In addition, this is something that you should emphasise at interview. Gossip and careless talk, even within the office environment is dangerous and simply not acceptable. We look at this in fuller detail in Chapter Four.

3.2.6 Staff appraisal

You will wish to take any new member of staff on a probationary period to begin with. You should be clear about the length of the probationary period when you take the new member of staff on. During that time you should build in review and training timers as all new staff need some support—even if they are very experienced they will need to know how you want things organised. Build into your management of your staff an annual appraisal system. Again you can buy books and software to guide you.

3.2.7 Staff meetings and communication

Also it is good practice to have regular staff meetings, either with individuals or as a group, or blend of the two. For example, each Tuesday morning may be dedicated to staff meetings and training. The first Tuesday of the month might be given over to a staff meeting of all staff, and in the intervening weeks you may set up a system for seeing the staff individually.

3.3 Practicalities

3.3.1 Health and Safety

All firms, no matter how small, have to comply with the health and safety laws. You have a duty of care with regard to health and safety for your employees, visiting workers, other visitors (probably clients in this case) and members of the general public. The rules apply to the safety of the premises as well as any risks arising from the work we do, counselling. An Inspector has the right to enter your premises at any time.

To comply fully with health and safety requirements you need to make sure that you have the following in place (if I have discussed any item fully elsewhere I will not discuss it here).

Employers' public liability insurance Covered in the insurance section. Briefly, it is the law that you must have Employers' Public Liability Insurance and that you display the certificate.

Risk assessment All employers and self-employed people have to assess the risks from their work activities. If you have more than five employees you have to record the significant findings of your risk assessment.

Safety policy If you have more than five employees then by law you must have a written health and safety policy.

Staff training   You must provide training for all staff in the area of Health and Safety. This includes:

Manual Handling Assessment—You need to make sure that you train all your staff on how to carry things and how to lift. To be on the safe side you should give all staff a written summary of the training you gave them on lifting (and ask them to sign it)—so many accidents at work are caused by lifting badly, even a parcel that comes in the post. Slipping or tripping at work causes the most common injuries—e.g. computer or electrical cables, extension leads that are not carefully secured. In the counselling business you may need to think about repetitive strain injury if your secretary spends too much time typing up reports. Make sure your computer is correctly set up, together with the desk and chair

Electricity at Work Regulations—You need to be sure that your electrical equipment is in good working order and that it is suitable for your working environment.

Fire Safety—You would be surprised at what we all have in our homes and offices that is flammable, e.g. petrol, paint thinner, packaging materials, dusts from wood, flour and sugar.

Fire Emergency Procedure—I suggest giving staff written instructions about what to do in the case of fire.

Fire Exit Signs and Exits—Make sure that you clearly sign the fire exits and that you inform all members of staff about the route to take.

Fire Extinguishers—You should make sure that you have fire extinguishers of the correct kind and big enough for your premises. For example you may need a separate foam extinguisher for use on electrical items. I suggest looking in Yellow Pages under Fire Extinguishing Equipment. Many companies will come and do an assessment, sell you the extinguishers (new or second hand) and maintain and inspect them annually for you for a small fee.

First Aid Box—You should keep a well-stocked first aid box. You can buy them from any chemist. Also you should appoint someone to take charge of first-aid arrangements. Do not hand out medication, even aspirin.

Accident Report Book—You should keep an accident report book—you can buy appropriate books from a stationers. You must record all accidents, however minor, and the date of the accident.

You should get a copy of "Everyone's guide to RIDDOR HSE31" (from the HSE www.hse.gov.uk/pubns/**hse31**.pdf) for more details of work place-related accidents, diseases and dangerous occurrences.

Health and Safety Law Poster—By law you need to display the health and safety poster at work (www.hsebooks.com).

Registration of Premises—If you employ anyone then you will need to register your premises with the local authority (usually the Environmental Health Department).

Inspectors from the Health and Safety Executive (HSE) or your local authority administer the health and safety laws. For a counselling business it is likely that the local authority will administer the laws. Inspectors visit the work place to check that people are sticking to the rules. They can be extremely helpful for advice.

Useful address: The HSE operate a confidential telephone helpline called Infoline on 0845 881 165. www.hse.gov.uk

You can order free booklets covering many of these areas from HSE on 01787 881 165.

Although this all sounds very serious and full of doom and gloom, in fact so long as you are sensible and set things up the right way, as a counselling business you will have few problems with health and safety. The one area that you will specifically need to think about is if a client becomes violent. Make sure you have an in-house policy for this before it happens. I will discuss this in Chapter Four in more detail.

Workbook Question and Answer Session:

Tick off this checklist as you implement each of the health and safety areas and where necessary write down your plans

- Employers' public liability insurance
- Risk assessment
- Staff training including Manual Handling Assessment
- Electricity at Work regulations
- Fire—including:
  - Fire safety
  - Fire emergency procedure
  - Fire exit signs and exits
  - Fire extinguishers
- First aid box
- Accident Report book
- Get a copy of "Everyone's guide to RIDDOR HSE31"
- Get a copy of the Health and Safety Law poster
- Registration of premises

When you have completed this section you will probably be totally exhausted—if not go on to the next section.

3.3.2 Premises

As a counsellor choosing your premises correctly is paramount. Premises and staff will be your two biggest costs so make sure, before you take on consulting rooms, that you can really afford them.

To check you can afford premises work out your Profit and Loss and your Cash Flow forecasts BEFORE signing leases or licences.

Do all your planning before getting premises—there are plenty of offices and suitable rooms available. Never think that the rooms you have seen are the only ones for you.

3.3.2.1 Premises checklist

Location   How do your clients come to you? If they come by car then think about road access, and parking but if they need to come on public transport is it going to be easy for them to get to you? At the end of the day bad location may put some clients off coming to you.

Layout   You will need to have at least one consulting room, a waiting area, a secretarial administration area, and possibly a coffee corner/kitchenette. Appearance is also important and you will need to give the right image.

Lease   Get a solicitor to check the lease—especially to make sure that you can carry on counselling from the premises.

- Are there rent reviews and when are they?
- Check the lease to see who is responsible for repairs and insurance. If you are responsible the repairs and main-tenance get a survey and negotiate a reduction based on the results.
- Check all the costings before signing anything, including running costs, repairs and alterations, business rates.

Viewing   When you look at a property I do recommend that you go and see it at different times of day and on different days. For example, a road may seem very quiet when you go at 10.00 am. But if you went back at 7.30 pm (when you may well be seeing clients) the noise of all the customers from the nearby fish and chip shop may drive you mad. Also, if you are in a residential area, in the day time there may be no parking, but by 6.00 pm there is not a space in sight for your clients.

Workbook Question and Answer Session:

Working out the best premises for your practice:

Location

Layout

Lease

Viewing

Planning permission

Sound

Safety

Planning permission   You will also need to make sure that you are allowed to use the premises as consulting rooms. If in doubt, consult the Local Authority—planning and building control officer.

Sound   Because of the nature of your work you need to be sure that your consulting room is sufficiently sound-proofed so that those in the waiting area and any reception/secretarial staff cannot hear anything. You also need to make sure that people cannot look into the room easily.

Safety   You need to consider your safety, the safety of your staff and of your clients.

3.3.2.2 *Renting versus buying*

You could search for premises and take out a lease. This would probably be for a minimum of 2/3 years and could be up to 20 years. You may not want to be held to such a commitment as a new business. You may be asked to give a personal guarantee in the event of the failure of your business. I strongly advise *not* giving such a guarantee. I suggest that you negotiate a break clause every 3 or 5 years in the lease. Signing a lease is easy, getting out of a lease is very difficult and could be very costly. I urge you to get good legal advice.

Rather less risky, you could look at serviced offices that provide different levels of back up, including telephone answering, photocopying. These are often let on a monthly basis. They are more expensive (but much less expensive than taking on a costly lease that you might not need) but will include things such as business rates, heating, service charges and rent. You would need to look carefully at suitability given your client group.

You may be able to find consulting rooms with others in allied professions. These can be really attractive as they add value to your business whilst also giving you waiting areas, security, back up etc.

Finally you may choose to purchase your premises. I would only recommend this if you have sufficient collateral at the beginning of your business. You can always buy some premises once you know that your business is a success.

3.3.2.3 *Working from home versus having your own premises*

Working from home has its advantages and its disadvantages. You will need to weigh up both before making a decision. Clients are quite used to going to a counsellor's home, but it can be quite an intrusion on your family. It can also be a distraction for you when you can hear your 2 year old screaming in the background.

You will need to include associated costs when you work out your costings. Whilst you will save on paying a rent you may have to pay business rates, which can be very steep. You may need to install a phone system, or have some redecorating. Make sure you include ALL your costs in your forecasts.

If you decide to work from home make sure you tell your mortgage company and home insurer (you may need to pay an extra premium).

3.3.2.4 *Equipment*

Fortunately you can start counselling with very little equipment. Just a couple of comfortable chairs will start you off. However, if you wish to set up a professional practice that gains a good reputation then you need to think carefully about the image you will give. Your choice of furniture and décor will say everything about you and your style of practice, as I discussed in Chapter One.

Remember, you do not have to buy everything new— there are plenty of second hand office furniture stores, which sell everything from armchairs to photocopiers. Before buying anything get prices from different suppliers and try to beat them down on price—remember every penny less than you pay is a penny more profit for you. Always get receipts as you can use these as expenses within the business to offset against tax.

Never pay cash for an item without getting a receipt. Without a receipt you will not have the proof that you bought the item and will not be able to put it through your accounts.

Most of all, remember you are going to spend a lot of your life in these consulting rooms—make sure you like them and can feel comfortable in them.

3.4 Protocols and procedures

When you start out you will probably do everything yourself, cleaning the toilets, making appointments, doing the accounts—and that's just for starters. You will be amazed by what a variety of tasks you develop competence in!

When you can afford to hire staff it will make a big difference if you have written summary sheets for each of the areas of business, for example, how to do the banking, how you like the telephone answered, computer back-up. This will mean that if you have a change-over of staff all is not lost as they are using your system not theirs and it should be seamless (in theory). Develop a system for filing these protocols so that staff can easily find them (not just in the recesses of your computer). Don't forget to update them from time-to-time.

3.5 Drawing together the threads

Think about our two examples, Donna with her group practice, and Simon, with his part-time practice. From the little you know about them, have they paid sufficient attention to the practicalities of the business, or have they concentrated on the counselling side?

For Simon, as a relatively small-timer—what particular aspects of the business is he going to struggle with?

What will you struggle with?

How can you overcome these obstacles?

Remember that to ignore them will have long-term consequences!

CHAPTER FOUR

Specific issues for a counselling business

Whatever you have been used to doing in your counselling work, you will need to do even better in private practice. You will need to be even more rigorous in your management and have the highest possible standards in your clinical practice. The feedback from insurers and professional organisations is that complaints are on the increase. In private practice you are more vulnerable because you are isolated and less well supported. This chapter looks at how we can overcome and minimise these problems and ensure that you are well equipped for private practice.

Private business is full of competition; your professional reputation will count for everything.

I want now to consider some issues that specifically arise for the private counsellor.

4.1 Money and collecting fees

One of the things practitioners hate the most is dealing with the MONEY! So often practitioners feel that it taints the psychological and psychotherapeutic process. Other practitioners see the money issue and collection as part of the process. Whatever your views, there are ways of making it easier for yourself by making some simple rules.

1   Put up a poster in your consulting room, or in the waiting area, letting people know about your Terms and Conditions— a bit like the dentist or the doctor—especially those relating to cancellation and payment. We discussed the Client Information Sheet in section 2.3.3—but this will include the Terms and Conditions. Here is an example:

Appointments
If you need to change an appointment we will be happy to do so providing you give us at least 24 hours' notice. If you need to cancel or change an appointment with less than 24 hours' notice we reserve the right to charge the full amount.

Payments
Billing is usually monthly, in advance. Payment is expected immediately on production of the invoice, by cash, cheque, or PayPal.

Full Terms and Conditions
Please ask your practitioner for our full Terms and Conditions.

---

2   Decide your policy on cancellations and stick to it. If people realise that you are not going to charge for cancellations you will be messed about far more than if you are strict about it.
3   Decide on how you are going to implement your payments procedures. What are you going to accept? Cash, credit cards (conventional or PayPal), cheque. Always give a receipt or invoice for which you keep a duplicate.

4   Decide when in the consulting session you are going to do the payments and appointments practicalities. I personally think it is better at the beginning of the session to book all future appointments and do the money. That way there is less risk of running out of time or muddling money and psychological issues. Personally I do appointments for four sessions at a time, which I invoice on the spot (you can use a duplicate invoice book so the client has a record of the agreed appointments and the payment all on one piece of paper). In other words, I receive the money upfront. This is good for your cash-flow, but also you will find that you get far fewer cancellations if people have already paid!

Workbook Question and Answer Session:

How am I going to plan my appointment booking system?

What is my policy on cancellations?

What is my policy on taking payment?

4.2 The contract between you and the client

The contract that you will have between you and the client will be on a number of levels including the legal and the psychological.

There are responsibilities on both sides, whether things are written or agreed verbally. But we all known it is far easier to enforce a written contract and my advice is to get everything in writing.

When you take on a client, this is the beginning of a contract; when a client gives you money this becomes legally binding.

See Appendix 6 for a sample Client Details and Agreement Form.

4.3 Isolation

As humans we are social creatures and many of us need the social interaction that going out to work gives us—counsellors are no exception. The world of work is, amongst other things, a social activity, which is why home working will never rule the world—we need other people for social contact. Working alone is not for everyone, and no matter how fine a counsellor or psychotherapist you may be, you may hate working alone. This is something you may only know after having tried it.

As counsellors we work in isolation a great deal of the time and we need to support ourselves to make sure this does not get to us. Working as a counsellor in an organisation is very different as we have meeting times, informal colleague support and the structure of the organisation to support us. All of that disappears when you set up your own practice.

You will need to be self-disciplined, plan your time, form your own networks and work out how you can best support yourself. This could be by meeting other counsellors working on their own for a discussion group, or by having a secretary/receptionist working for you (NB costs). Networking with peers can have a useful secondary role as you can use such meetings to share ideas and difficulties you all share, to undertake further group study in a particular field, or for peer supervision.

Wookbook Question and Answer Session:

Am I (honestly) cut out to work alone?

If the answer is yes, then how can I develop networks and supports to avoid getting isolated?

4.4 Trust, good quality of care and codes of ethics

The BACP's ethical framework for good practice in counselling and psychotherapy gives guidance and boundaries for a number of areas which I believe ultimately boil down to the client being able to trust you, your judgement, your actions and your knowledge. With this comes knowing the limits of your competence, working within an ethical framework, not doing (intentionally or unintentionally) harm to your client. And much more.

You will no doubt be following a code of ethics. If you are not, to be blunt, you should not be working in counselling and psychotherapy. I do not intend to discuss the full issues of codes of ethics as these are things you will have learned in your training. I will highlight only those which have a particular bearing on private practice.

Remember in your private practice you will be the boss, and will at times have to make weighty and sometimes unpleasant decisions. You need to ensure you are well informed. Ignorance is no defence.

4.5 Reputation

Anything you can do to make your name known will help build your practice. I have already discussed this in detail in Chapter One, but if you have some specific interests within counselling, such as bereavement counselling, AIDS counselling, or working with children, then use this interest to best effect: write papers for journals, undertake a simple research project, develop a local interest group, get on the circuit for giving lectures on the subject. All these are ways of getting yourself known, keeping your reputation at the forefront of people's minds and developing your name within the local community.

4.6 Dual relationships and conflicts of interest

Talking of local communities—one of the problems of working in a local community is that you will bump into your clients in the supermarket, or at a drinks party, or at the sports centre. You may wish to develop your practice a little away from where you live. Either way, you need to work out strategies for how you will deal with these eventualities.

You need to be crystal clear about conflicts in relationship roles as this can lead to much heartache. These are often called dual relationships and can be when a supervisor is also your lecturer, or a good friend asks you for counselling help, or intense sexual feelings arise between you and the client. Don't think these issues won't arise for you—they will!

> **Example**
> Josephine has a part-time counselling practice and during the other half of her working life she works as an accounts clerk in the local factory. She uses her maiden name for her

counselling work. One day a lady called Marion phones up to book a first appointment and although Josephine picks up that the lady had a voice that was familiar to her she didn't think anything of it. Both Josephine and Marion were embarrassed when Marion came for her first appointment and it turns out they worked together.

Both being adult about the situation, they looked at the options available and eventually Marion went on to see a colleague of Josephine. Josephine will also need to retain confidentiality about the issues raised by Marion on the telephone in their initial conversation.

How would you have coped with this situation?

What measures can you put in place . . .

a) to prevent it happening?

b) when it occurs?

You need to think very hard about any such relationship as they can be very damaging for both client and counsellor—but here your concern must be first and foremost the welfare of your client.

4.7 Confidentiality

Many people follow the BACP "Ethical framework for good practice in counselling and psychotherapy". As part of your chosen code of ethics you will be required to maintain confidentiality. You need to be crystal clear what confidentiality means to you and when you will need to break it. Ideally this should only be with the agreement of your client, but there are times when legally you will need to break confidentiality.

Roger Litton lists a number of areas where issues of confidentiality will be ethically troubling:

- *Risk to third parties*—sexual abuse, other child abuse and neglect, threatened violence, HIV.
- *Risk to the client*—threatened suicide.
- *Disclosure of information to others*—particularly to medical agencies, other colleagues, close friends, relatives.
- *Pressure to disclose*—he uses the example of working in an organisational setting where there may be conflicting pressures between financial management and the therapy room management.
- *Careless/inappropriate disclosure*—by the psychotherapist or others.

Confidentiality is linked to trust, and in my experience when you talk to clients about your concerns about them or their problems they will usually agree with what you suggest, whether it is regarding contacting the GP, or getting a second opinion, or even, social services if you were worried about child abuse. It is far better to work with your client's agreement and knowledge—preferably getting their agreement in writing. They will also learn to trust you if you are very clear about the boundaries. If you work in this way you will probably never have to breach confidentiality.

As I have said elsewhere, you will need to be sure that any staff you employ FULLY understand this requirement and can keep it 100%, as it is inevitable that from time to time they will pick things up.

Confidentiality is a huge area that is as relevant to the organisational practitioner as to the private practice practitioner. What is different is that all the decisions are down to you. If you need more advice on confidentiality I suggest *Confidentiality and the Law* by Roger Litton, Mark Scroggins and Stephen Palmer which teases out the important issues. For the private practitioner what is key is that you get good professional indemnity insurance.

4.8 Record keeping and note-taking

4.8.1 Security

As a professional, I believe that you should make notes. However, because of the increases in litigation there has been a move away from keeping process noting, to factual recording of the sessions. Remember that whatever notes you make may be called up in a court of law. I always tell my clients how I make notes, and how they will be stored for security. It is important that you are consistent in your note-taking as you may need at a later date to use them, for example if you are called as an expert witness. It is quite a good idea to include your supervision record with the notes as this shows that you have reflected on the particular case.

You will need to keep your records in a secure setting. You should make notes after each session, and these should be made in black pen (not pencil). The reason for this is a bit sad, but litigation is increasing. Black pen is the most durable colour, pencil notes could be altered. Make sure you date your notes each time.

If you want to computerise your records I recommend that you do not store them on the hard disk, but on a floppy disk that you can lock away. You should ensure that you reformat your disks after usage, not just erase the files as there will still be traceable files with the appropriate software.

You should code your records, rather than using full names, so that they are not easily identifiable if seen by someone else.

You should print out all your computerised records in case of disk failure and keep them in a locked place as well.

You may want to consider buying a small desktop shredder for destroying any confidential documents and notes.

If you are called upon to provide your notes—you should not automatically do so. You should only disclose your notes in response to a valid order or reason, for example as a result of a court order, a request from a statutory agency. You do not need to disclose information just because, for example, a solicitor, a police officer, or other professional may ask for it.

You should check with your professional body how best to keep your records and what the law requires of those notes.

I asked a colleague who is expert in this area what her views were—and this was her anonymous reply:

> Anything filed specifically under a client's name or code, particularly on a computer, might be seen to be medical records and the client can ask to see them. My advice is that *all notes* should be headed 'For discussion in supervision' in one colour pen and then have the odd jotting from self, peer or paid supervision at the bottom. In the hell in our house X was saved from having to release her notes until now because the Information Commissioner deemed them to be notes of a conversation with a third party and not medical records/case notes.

This area is a minefield, not limited to the world of private practice. Hopefully you will have covered the latest legal position within your course when you trained or updated more recently with CPD.

4.8.2 The Data Protection Act 1984 and 1998

The Data Protection Acts are designed to protect the public regarding confidentiality and junk mail. Originally the 1984 Act applies only to computerised records, but now that remit has been extended to individual paper records.

To work out whether you should register with the Data Protection Register you can fill in a questionnaire on line: http://forms.informationcommissioner.gov.uk/notify/self/question1.html

Useful address: Data Protection Registrar, Wycliffe House, Water Lane, Wilmslow, Cheshire SK9 5AF; Website: http://www.cfoi.org.uk and http://www.open.gov.uk/dpr/dprhome.htm

4.9 Complaints

We have already looked at this under insurance, confidentiality and record-keeping. However, as there is so much concern about this area I wish to make some suggestions here. In addition Anne Kearn's new book *Complaints, Litigation and Good Practice: Protecting Yourself and Developing Healthy Practice*, due out 2006 is ESSENTIAL reading, especially if you think that you are not at risk!

There are some very simple things you can do to help yourself if there is a complaint.

1   Consult your professionals body as quickly as possible.
2   Discuss the complaint in supervision.
3   Read around the subject.
4   Read your code of ethics before you start your practice. If you hit a problem, reread it. Ensure that everything you do lies, to the best of your ability, within the confines of the code.
5   Keep notes—you will be keeping notes in any case, but if you suspect there is a problem lurking, ensure that you make detailed notes of everything you do, including dates of phone calls and what was said.
6   Make sure you are insured from the outset, as insurance will not cover an existing problem—and also talk to your insurer.

4.10 Illness, death or critical emergency

You will need to decide a policy with a trusted member of staff or a colleague about what should happen if you were ill or, heaven forbid, you should die. You need to make arrangements in such an event for someone to cancel your appointments, and if necessary to destroy your records. It is wise to let your client know what arrangements you make—I have heard one or two horror stories—counsellors and therapists do die and we need to acknowledge the damage that this can do to a client if they are not sensitively informed.

4.11 Audit

Every area of professional work involves assessment of one kind or another. The word audit frightens people—we think of accountants who audit a business, they check their figures. Counselling audit is a great deal less precise but the process of audit ensures that we are carrying out our practice to the highest standards within the current available knowledge.

Useful article: Ann Thomas (1996) "Clinical Audit: setting professional standards for counselling services", *Counselling Psychology Quarterly*, 9(1): 25–36.

I am sure that if you are working in the NHS you are quite used to this process. In private practice it is even more important. Peer review can be a useful way of auditing your work—it also helps with the isolation. In peer review you audit each other's work. The important element here is that it is a two-way process.

4.12 Information sheet and your arrangements

I would urge you to consider if preparing a simple information sheet that you give all prospective and new clients. It could include the following:

- Your full name
- Your business address and telephone number
- Your qualifications and training
- Your Code of Ethics
- Your supervision arrangements
- Membership of any professional organisations (be careful not to misrepresent your memberships)
- Your experience
- How you work—initial assessment interview, planning of sessions, review sessions, ending therapy, how long the sessions last
- Days and times you are available for appointment
- How psychotherapy or counselling may help you
- In what circumstances you would need to break confidentiality
- Arrangements for being contacted in a client emergency (e.g. times)
- Accreditation details
- What happens if you get ill or die
- Payments details—when, how much and how they should pay, and cancellation terms
- Methods of payment accepted
- Travel details—stations, buses, parking

This sheet could be combined with the Terms and Conditions mentioned in section 2.3.3. You might wish to call it something more gentle, such as "Information Sheet"!

4.13 Professional regulation

Whilst some progress has been made towards regulation of the profession, this is still in the melting pot with a date of 2008 being considered for statutory regulation.

Currently, whilst there are some requirements for those who adhere to Codes of Ethics, the whole field of Counselling and Psychotherapy is wide open—anyone can call themselves a counsellor with little or no training, and this does huge disservice to those of us who have taken our training very seriously provide a high standard of service.

Whilst the profession is gradually addressing these issues, it is not there yet. All you can do is to maintain the highest standards of practice, including your supervision, continuing professional development, adherence to a Code of Practice. Within the remit I would expect you to continue your personal therapy on at least some formal basis, and to engage in at least adequate supervision for the amount of clients you are seeing, in line with the Code of Ethics that you adhere to.

4.14 Registration, accreditation and chartership

Only psychology as a profession has fully achieved chartership— no one may call themselves a psychologist unless chartered through the British Psychological Society. Our time will come in both counselling and psychotherapy. No matter where we practise we need to constantly maintain the highest standards in our work. Accreditation and registration will never weed out bad counsellors and therapists, but for the majority, it aims to give us a minimum focus that we should achieve, whilst to some extent protecting the general public.

In preparation for statutory registration getting the highest qualifications and accreditation will prepare you as fully as possible making you eligible for statutory registration.

4.15 Continuing professional development

Continuing professional development is another important plank of our personal development as career counsellors and psychotherapists. All professionals need to update their knowledge even if it is not a statutory requirement of counselling yet. You can often use these courses towards your accreditation, should you need to, and the cost of the courses can be offset against tax. I find a lot of counsellors go to conferences—another way of networking and undertaking your continuing professional development at the same time.

Continuing professional development (CPD) is very important as a way of ensuring that we continue to provide the highest quality of informed practice.

4.16 Professional memberships

In private practice you will need to be seen to be successful and to be a key member of the counselling community. One way of developing this reputation is by becoming a member of professional organisations and, if appropriate, business clubs. You might want to develop some links with local psychiatry services, even if it means having to offer your services on a voluntary capacity for a few hours a week—all this looks good on an information sheet and adds to your networking and referral resources. Remember you can offset these costs against tax.

4.17 Referral systems

Referral pathways are singularly important for you as the private practitioner. I have said a lot about isolation—professionally you can be completely isolated. It is essential that you build up a network of other professionals locally to whom you can refer and confer. In particular a friendly GP will be invaluable, as will a psychiatrist to whom you can send people for a second opinion. You may find your books are full and that you need to give other names of counsellors—I never feel comfortable giving the name of a counsellor unless I personally know them and have confidence in their abilities.

However in addition to all these reasons, there will be times when you are uncomfortable or unwilling to take on a client. We all have chinks in our personalities or/and life histories and there will most certainly be times when we will need to take great care.

Building a good multi-professional and multi-agency referral network will be very important—it is important to do this work as soon as possible rather than reacting to a situation when it arises—it's called planning!!

Confidentiality will of course be extremely important when working with other agencies or referring on to other agencies. You will want to get your client's permission. I personally like to give a copy to the client and agree the letter with them, but that is a personal choice. Try to keep your letters short and factual—especially if you are writing to a doctor.

When writing a referral letter don't forget to include the following information:

- Client's contact details
- How the client came to you in the first instance and their presenting problem
- A brief history of their background
- What the client's current difficulties are
- Any medication and treatment (physical or psychological)
- What psychotherapeutic or counselling treatment they have received from you and what you think they need

4.18 Assessment

It is ironic that I should nearly finish this book with assessment, which is where we as professional counsellors need to start in our practice. It is easy to get sloppy in private practice. The work of assessment is even more important to the private practitioner—as much for your protection as for that of the client.

You will, I hope, have been trained in assessment techniques as part of your basic training. If not, it is time for your first Continuing Professional Development course that you will be able to offset against tax! Good assessment is the key to good practice, whether within your care or as a referral on to another agency.

You may wish to devise an initial form that clients fill in before they come to you, or you may wish to use the first session to gain some of this information. You will need to take very detailed notes at this point. Some counsellors prefer to tape their sessions to help with their note writing (remember these count as records and may be called upon in any legal proceedings). The choice is yours but you should talk about how and why you do this with your client.

I enclose a possible start point for an assessment form in Appendix 5.

4.19 Drawing together the threads

Thinking about our two examples, Donna with her group practice, and Simon, with his part-time practice, what are the issues that arise in Chapter 4 that are going to be difficult for Simon. Will it be professional loneliness? Will it be boundary issues living in the same community in which he works? Will it be the financial drain that can go with Continuing Professional Development and membership costs? How can he surmount these hurdles?

CHAPTER FIVE

Working self-employed within the NHS

The title of this chapter sounds like a contradiction of terms. However, there are a number of counsellors in this situation.

Advising in this area is difficult as the ground rules are permanently changing. My advice is not to get into the position of being self-employed within the NHS if you can avoid it as it is not in your long-term interest, although you may initially feel richer!

As a self-employed person you have to comply with the law. A number of NHS Trusts and Primary Care Trusts would prefer for you to be self-employed and for you to invoice them at regular intervals. They will want to do this as this keeps down PAYE and National Insurance bills and they do not have the same duty of care to a contractor as to a member of their salaried staff. *In other words, they may be getting you cheap and with less protection for you and will not have your best interests in mind.*

There are some criteria about whether you can work self-employed or not:

If YOU determined: your level of pay
the hours you work
and whether the place of work is varied or
your home

If you fulfill these criteria (and most of you will not) you may be able to work self-employed as you are in control of these items.

If the Trust determines these items, for example, how much you are paid, etc. then you will be deemed to be an employee and the Inland Revenue can follow up on both you and the Trust for non-payment of tax.

CPCs (Counsellors and Psychotherapists in Primary Care) advice is as follows:

> Our current understanding is that if a counsellor is employed for a fixed number of hours each week on a fixed hourly rate that constitutes employment. Working part-time is not relevant to the definition of employed status. Reference should be made to the Inland Revenue's document: "Employed or Self-Employed?" IR56/N139 (7). As PCTs are legal bodies they are able to employ staff. Furthermore the introduction and implementation of Agenda For Change in 2004 as a single schema NHS pay system and the consequent inclusion in A4C of counsellors in the pay bands and job definitions alongside other health professionals means that locally agreed terms and conditions for counsellors are no longer sustainable in the long term. Thanks to considerable work by CPC in partnership with Amicus, counsellors are now part of the NHS as defined by the A4C job bandings, spine points and structured career progression (see appendices A and B).
>
> (Foster, J. and Murphy, A.)

In other words, resist self-employment if possible!

To summarise, it is usually in your interests to be an employee rather than self-employed as the terms and conditions of your work will be much better with supervision, sick pay, pensions, holidays and other items considered within the terms.

Think very carefully before entering into a self-employed relationship with a Trust unless you are carrying out a one-off contract such as delivery of a lecture. Self-employment in the NHS will result in uncertainty as the contractual obligation is vague and you will have no security of contract.

CPC has some questions that are particularly relevant regarding self-employment in their *Guidance and Frameworks for a Managed Primary Care Counselling Service* (J. Foster, and A. Murphy, 2004). For example:

- Who owns the patients' notes and where are they stored?
- Will you be signed up to the Children Act in terms of Child Protection?
- What happens if there is a complaint?

The law, and practice relating to the law is constantly changing. I therefore recommend that you contact CPC if you find yourself in these circumstances to ensure that you sign up to best practice and also what is best for you in the long term.

Useful address: CPC, Queensway House, Queensway, Bognor Regis, West Sussex, PO21 1QT. Tel: 01243 870701, cpc@ **cpc-online**.co.uk

5.1 Drawing together the threads

Thinking about our two examples, Donna with her group practice, and Simon, with his part-time practice, what would be the best contractual arrangements if Donna's partnership were to provide a counselling service with a local NHS Trust?

What if Simon was approached by his local GP to do 5 hours a week in the GP surgery—how should he proceed? Should he accept self-employed terms or should he stick out for a proper contract? What are the advantages and disadvantages? What would you do in Simon's situation?

REFERENCES AND SUGGESTED READING

Foster, J., & Murphy, A. (2004). *Guidance and Frameworks for a Managed Primary Care Counselling Service*. Bognor Regis: CPC.

Kearns, A. (2006). *The Mirror Crack'd—when things go wrong in counselling and psychotherapy, and other cautionary tales*. London: Karnac.

Litton, R., Palmer, S., & Scroggins, M. (2001). *Confidentiality and the Law*. In: P. Milner, & S. Palmer (Eds.). *Counselling: The BACP Counselling Reader*, Volume 2. London: Sage Publications in association with BACP.

McMahon, G., Palmer, S., & Wilding, C. (2005). *The Essential Skills for Setting up a Counselling and Psychotherapy Practice*. Hove: Routledge.

Thomas, A. (1996). Clinical Audit: setting professional standards for counselling services. *Counselling Psychology Quarterly*, 9(1): 25–36.

Webster, M. (2005). *The Director's Handbook: your duties, responsibilities and liabilities*. London: Director Publications.

Useful organisations

Organisation	Its role	Address	Contact details
Association of Chartered Certified Accountants (ACCA)		ACCA Connect 2 Central Quay 89 Hydepark Street Glasgow G3 8DT	0141 582 2000 info@accaglobal.com www.accaglobal.com
British Association for Counselling and Psychotherapy (BACP)	Professional membership organisation for counsellors and psychotherapists	BACP House 35–37 Albert Street Rugby Warwickshire CV21 2SG	0870 443 5252 bacp@bacp.co.uk www.bacp.co.uk
British Psychological Society (BPS)	Professional membership organisation for psychologists	St. Andrew's House 48 Princess Road East Leicester LE1 7DR	0116 254 9568 enquiry@bps.org.uk www.bps.org.uk
Companies Registration Office (England and Wales)	The official UK government register of UK companies	Companies House Crown Way Cardiff CF4 3UZ	01222 388 588 www.companieshouse.gov.uk
Confederation of Scottish Counselling Agencies (COSCA)	The professional body for counselling and psychotherapy in Scotland	18 Viewfield Street Stirling FK8 1UA	01786 475140 info@cosca.org.uk www.cosca.org.uk
Counsellors and Psychotherapists in Primary Care (CPC)	The specialist professional membership organisation representing counsellors in primary care	Queensway House Queensway Bognor Regis West Sussex PO21 1QT	01243 870701 cpc@cpc-online.co.uk www.cpc-online.co.uk

Organisation	Address	Contact
Data Protection Registrar	Wycliffe House Water Lane Wilmslow SK9 5AF	01625 545 745 (enq) 01625 535 711 (admin) www.dataprotection.gov.uk
DTI	Publications Orderline Admail 528 London SW1W 8YT	0870 150 2500 http://www.dti.gov.uk/publications
European Association of Counselling	*Secretary:* Jenny Anagnostopoulos PO Box 78017 Ag. Dimitrios 17310 Athens Greece	+30 210 975 6047 eac@hol.gr www.eacnet.org
European Association of Psychotherapy	The EAP represents 128 organisations (24 national umbrella associations, 17 European-wide associations for psychotherapy) from 41 European countries and by that more than 120,000 psychotherapists. Membership is also open for individual psychotherapists Sonja Wirgler EAP Head Office Schnirchgasse 9a 4th Floor/room 410 1030 Vienna Austria	+43 1 5131729 eap.headoffice@europsyche.org www.europsyche.org
Federation of Small Businesses	To improve standards of business and to represent small businesses politically	01253 336000 www.fsb.org.uk

Organisation	Its role	Address	Contact details
Health & Safety Executive			0845 881 1650845 881 165 www.hse.gov.uk
Health & Safety Executive Books	Excellent publications for business start-up and items such as HSE obligatory poster for sale		01787 881 165 www.hsebooks.com
HM Revenue & Customs	This is an excellent site to get the latest on National Insurance, employment, self-assessment, VAT, taxes, being an employer and lots more		http://www.hmrc.gov.uk/
ICOM	ICOM is the Industrial Common Ownership Movement Limited, a non-profit membership organisation promoting and representing democratic employee-owned businesses throughout the UK	Holyoake House Hanover Street Manchester M60 0AS	0161 246 2959 icom@icom.org.uk www.icof.co.uk/icom
Institute of Chartered Accountants in England & Wales		Chartered Accountants' Hall PO Box 433 London EC2P 2BJ	020 7920 8100 www.icaew.co.uk

Institute of Directors	To improve standards of business and to represent business politically—you need to run a limited company for membership	www.iod.com
Irish Association for Counselling and Therapy (IACT)		01 2300061 iact@irish-counselling.ie www.irish-counselling.ie
Lawyers for Business Helpline		0171 405 9075
PlanIt Business Suite	Software for all your personnel needs	PlanIt Software Ltd 75 Wadham Road London SW15 2YR www.planit.co.uk
Philippa Weitz Training	In-house training on all aspects of mental health, including setting up a business and private practice	26 Church Road Portslade East Sussex BN41 1LA 020 8133 1322 info@PWTraining.com www.PWTraining.com
Rotary International	A great place to meet new contacts and get known. The basis of Rotary is service above self. It is an organization of professional business men and women	www.rotary.org

Organisation	Its role	Address	Contact details
Professional Insurance	Professional liability insurance for complementary therapists		Contact your professional body for details of recommended insurers
United Kingdom Council for Psychotherapy (UKCP)	Professional membership organisation for psychotherapists	2nd Floor Edward House 2 Wakley Street London EC1V 7LT	020 7014 9955 info@psychotherapy.org.uk www.psychotherapy.org.uk
VistaPrint	A quick but slightly expensive way of getting your business stationery and business cards quickly and easily. You just design everything on-line.		www.vistaprint.co.uk
Wilson Sanford	Chartered Accountants. The senior partner, Robin Wilson, kindly proofread this book for accounting accuracy.	85 Church Road Hove BN3 2BB	01273 821 441 hove@wilsonsandford.co.uk www.wilsonsandford.co.uk
Yell.com	Web-based business directory enquiries		Yell.com

Profit and Loss forecasts

Profit and Loss for a modest counselling business with between four and eight clients

	01-May-06	01-Jun-06	01-Jul-06	01-Aug-06	01-Sep-06
SALES (Note 1)					
Clients @ £40 per hour	£960.00	£840.00	£600.00	£420.00	£960.00
Teaching on college course	£400.00	£400.00	£400.00	£400.00	£400.00
Giving supervision @ £50 per hour	£250.00	£250.00	£250.00	£80.00	£160.00
Miscellaneous income for articles in magazines		£100.00			£300.00
TOTAL INCOME (A)	£1,610.00	£1,590.00	£1,250.00	£900.00	£1,820.00
EXPENDITURE (B)					
Salary/personal drawings	£500.00	£500.00	£500.00	£500.00	£500.00
Administration salary	£0.00	£0.00	£0.00	£0.00	£0.00
Pensions/insurance	£80.00	£80.00	£80.00	£80.00	£80.00
Rent	£0.00	£0.00	£0.00	£0.00	£0.00
Light/heating	£40.00	£40.00	£40.00	£40.00	£40.00
Telephone	£50.00	£50.00	£50.00	£50.00	£50.00
Business rates	£0.00	£0.00	£0.00	£0.00	£0.00
Business insurance	£20.00	£20.00	£20.00	£20.00	£20.00
Travel	£70.00	£70.00	£70.00	£70.00	£70.00
Motor insurance	£40.00	£40.00	£40.00	£40.00	£40.00
Motor running	£60.00	£60.00	£60.00	£60.00	£60.00
Motor repairs	£50.00	£50.00	£50.00	£50.00	£50.00
Bank charges	£15.00	£15.00	£15.00	£15.00	£15.00
Post and carriage	£5.00	£5.00	£5.00	£5.00	£5.00
Printing and publishing	£500.00	£0.00	£0.00	£0.00	£0.00
Office supplies	£100.00	£20.00	£20.00	£20.00	£20.00
Professional fees	£50.00	£50.00	£50.00	£50.00	£50.00
Repairs and renewals	£50.00	£50.00	£50.00	£50.00	£50.00
Advertising	£100.00	£100.00	£100.00	£100.00	£100.00
Miscellaneous	£50.00	£50.00	£50.00	£50.00	£50.00
Total	£1,780.00	£1,200.00	£1,200.00	£1,200.00	£1,200.00
Monthly Profit/Loss	−£170.00	£390.00	£50.00	−£300.00	£620.00
Carried forward P/L	−£170.00	£220.00	£270.00	−£30.00	£590.00

This Profit and Loss forecast demonstrates that having four to eight clients can be profitable if premises and reception staff are not hired and some other costs are scaled down.

01-Oct-06	01-Nov-06	01-Dec-06	01-Jan-07	01-Feb-07	01-Mar-07	01-Apr-07	TOTALS
£960.00	£1,120.00	£840.00	£960.00	£1,120.00	£1,120.00	£960.00	£10,860.00
£400.00	£400.00	£400.00	£400.00	£400.00	£400.00	£400.00	£4,800.00
£250.00	£250.00	£180.00	£180.00	£250.00	£250.00	£240.00	£2,590.00
		£50.00					£450.00
£1,610.00	£1,770.00	£1,470.00	£1,540.00	£1,770.00	£1,770.00	£1,600.00	£18,700.00
£500.00	£500.00	£500.00	£500.00	£500.00	£500.00	£500.00	£6,000.00
£0.00	£0.00	£0.00	£0.00	£0.00	£0.00	£0.00	£0.00
£80.00	£80.00	£80.00	£80.00	£80.00	£80.00	£80.00	£960.00
£0.00	£0.00	£0.00	£0.00	£0.00	£0.00	£0.00	£0.00
£40.00	£40.00	£40.00	£40.00	£40.00	£40.00	£40.00	£480.00
£50.00	£50.00	£50.00	£50.00	£50.00	£50.00	£50.00	£600.00
£0.00	£0.00	£0.00	£0.00	£0.00	£0.00	£0.00	£0.00
£20.00	£20.00	£20.00	£20.00	£20.00	£20.00	£20.00	£240.00
£70.00	£70.00	£70.00	£70.00	£70.00	£70.00	£70.00	£840.00
£40.00	£40.00	£40.00	£40.00	£40.00	£40.00	£40.00	£480.00
£60.00	£60.00	£60.00	£60.00	£60.00	£60.00	£60.00	£720.00
£50.00	£50.00	£50.00	£50.00	£50.00	£50.00	£50.00	£600.00
£15.00	£15.00	£15.00	£15.00	£15.00	£15.00	£15.00	£180.00
£5.00	£5.00	£5.00	£5.00	£5.00	£5.00	£5.00	£60.00
£0.00	£200.00	£0.00	£0.00	£0.00	£0.00	£0.00	£700.00
£20.00	£20.00	£20.00	£20.00	£20.00	£20.00	£20.00	£320.00
£50.00	£50.00	£50.00	£50.00	£50.00	£50.00	£50.00	£600.00
£50.00	£50.00	£50.00	£50.00	£50.00	£50.00	£50.00	£600.00
£100.00	£100.00	£100.00	£100.00	£100.00	£100.00	£100.00	£1,200.00
£50.00	£50.00	£50.00	£50.00	£50.00	£50.00	£50.00	£600.00
£1,200.00	£1,400.00	£1,200.00	£1,200.00	£1,200.00	£1,200.00	£1,200.00	£15,180.00
£410.00	£370.00	£270.00	£340.00	£570.00	£570.00	£400.00	£3,520.00
£1,000.00	£1,370.00	£1,640.00	£1,980.00	£2,550.00	£3,120.00	£3,520.00	

Cash Flow Forecast for a modest counselling business with between four and eight clients

	01-May-06	01-Jun-06	01-Jul-06	01-Aug-06	01-Sep-06
SALES (Note 1)					
Clients @ £40 per hour	£500.00	£1,000.00	£800.00	£750.00	£760.00
Teaching on college course			£1,200.00		
Giving supervision @ £50 per hour		£400.00	£300.00	£80.00	£200.00
Misc income for articles in magazines		£100.00			£100.00
TOTAL INCOME (A)	£500.00	£1,500.00	£2,300.00	£830.00	£1,060.00
EXPENDITURE (B)					
Salary/personal drawings		£800.00	£700.00	£500.00	£500.00
Administration salary	£0.00	£0.00	£0.00	£0.00	£0.00
Pensions/insurance		£80.00	£80.00	£80.00	£80.00
Rent	£0.00	£0.00	£0.00	£0.00	£0.00
Light/heating			£120.00		
Telephone			£130.00		
Business rates	£0.00	£0.00	£0.00	£0.00	£0.00
Business insurance	£240.00				
Travel	£70.00	£70.00	£70.00	£70.00	£70.00
Motor insurance	£120.00			£120.00	
Motor running	£60.00	£60.00	£60.00	£60.00	£60.00
Motor repairs				£500.00	
Bank charges	£15.00	£15.00	£15.00	£15.00	£15.00
Post and carriage	£5.00	£5.00	£5.00	£5.00	£5.00
Printing and publishing	£0.00	£500.00	£0.00	£0.00	£0.00
Office supplies	£100.00	£20.00	£20.00	£20.00	£20.00
Professional fees	£300.00				
Repairs and renewals	£50.00	£50.00	£50.00	£50.00	£50.00
Advertising	£100.00	£100.00	£100.00	£100.00	£100.00
Miscellaneous	£50.00	£50.00	£50.00	£50.00	£50.00
Total	£1,110.00	£1,750.00	£1,400.00	£1,570.00	£950.00
Monthly Profit/Loss	−£610.00	−£250.00	£900.00	−£740.00	£110.00
Carried Forward P/L	−£610.00	−£860.00	£40.00	−£700.00	−£590.00

This Profit and Loss forecast demonstrates that having four to eight clients can be profitable if premises and reception staff are not hired and some other costs are scaled down.

01-Oct-06	01-Nov-06	01-Dec-06	01-Jan-07	01-Feb-07	01-Mar-07	01-Apr-07	TOTALS
£800.00	£850.00	£900.00	£1,300.00	£1,120.00	£1,120.00	£960.00	£10,860.00
	£1,200.00				£1,200.00	£1,200.00	£4,800.00
£400.00	£250.00	£220.00		£200.00	£300.00	£240.00	£2,590.00
£200.00			£25.00	£25.00			£450.00
£1,400.00	£2,300.00	£1,120.00	£1,325.00	£1,345.00	£2,620.00	£2,400.00	£18,700.00
£500.00	£500.00	£500.00	£500.00	£500.00	£500.00	£500.00	£6,000.00
£0.00	£0.00	£0.00	£0.00	£0.00	£0.00	£0.00	£0.00
£80.00	£80.00	£80.00	£80.00	£80.00	£80.00	£160.00	£960.00
£0.00	£0.00	£0.00	£0.00	£0.00	£0.00	£0.00	£0.00
	£210.00			£150.00			£480.00
£250.00			£100.00			£120.00	£600.00
£0.00	£0.00	£0.00	£0.00	£0.00	£0.00	£0.00	£0.00
							£240.00
£70.00	£70.00	£70.00	£70.00	£70.00	£70.00	£70.00	£840.00
	£120.00			£120.00			£480.00
£60.00	£60.00	£60.00	£60.00	£60.00	£60.00	£60.00	£720.00
				£100.00			£600.00
£15.00	£15.00	£15.00	£15.00	£15.00	£15.00	£15.00	£180.00
£5.00	£5.00	£5.00	£5.00	£5.00	£5.00	£5.00	£60.00
£0.00	£200.00	£0.00	£0.00	£0.00	£0.00	£0.00	£700.00
£20.00	£20.00	£20.00	£20.00	£20.00	£20.00	£20.00	£320.00
	£300.00						£600.00
£50.00	£50.00	£50.00	£50.00	£50.00	£50.00	£50.00	£600.00
£100.00	£100.00	£100.00	£100.00	£100.00	£100.00	£100.00	£1,200.00
£50.00	£50.00	£50.00	£50.00	£50.00	£50.00	£50.00	£600.00
£1,200.00	£1,780.00	£950.00	£1,050.00	£1,320.00	£950.00	£1,150.00	£15,180.00
£200.00	£520.00	£170.00	£275.00	£25.00	£1,670.00	£1,250.00	
−£390.00	£130.00	£300.00	£575.00	£600.00	£2,270.00	£3,520.00	

How to set up your accounts

ID	Date	Pd Date	Inv No	Description	Company	Method of paying	Expenditure total
1	03/02/2006	03/02/2006	56	JJ counselling 1/5, 18/5, 15/5, 22/5	JJ	Midland 346798	
2	03/02/2006	01/03/2006		Directory	British Association for Counselling	CASH	£20.00
3	03/02/2006	03/02/2006		Purchase of telephones	The Telecom Company	Cheque no: 000143	£80.00
4	03/02/2006	03/02/2006		Petrol	Palace S/S	CASH	£13.07
5	03/02/2006	01/03/2006		Counselling books	Dillons	VISA 4929 885 175 483	£14.98
6	03/02/2006	03/02/2006		Travelling to supervision	British Rail	CASH	£1.70
7	03/02/2006	03/02/2006		Petrol	Truckhaven Ltd	AMEX	£5.01
8	03/02/2006	01/03/2006		Telephone bill	One 2 One	Direct Debit from bus acc	£30.08
9	03/02/2006	01/03/2006	57	PJ counselling 23/5, 30/5	PJ	NatWest 000012	
10	03/02/2006	01/03/2006		Membership	British Association for Counselling	Cheque no: 000144	£58.00
11	03/02/2006	03/02/2006		Car servicing	DJ Autos	Cheque no: 000145	£129.23
12	03/02/2006	03/02/2006		Meal during colleague meeting	D'Plaza	VISA 4929 885 175 483	£23.00
13	03/02/2006	03/02/2006		Stamps	Post Office Counters	Cheque no: 000146	£100.00
14	03/02/2006	01/03/2006		Journal	Cruse Bereavement Care	Cheque no: 000147	£15.00
15	03/02/2006	03/02/2006		Monthly drawings	Philippa Weitz	Direct Debit to 0135321	£500.00
				Totals			£990.07
	The date on the invoice/receipt.	The date the payment goes through the bank.	Your invoice numbers.	Give enough detail so that the accountant/IR can identify the item.	When receiving income from client think about confidentiality as you will need to put their full details on the invoices/receipts you give them.	Identify HOW you paid and how you were paid.	Put all expenditure in this column and allocate it also to ONE other expenditure column. When checking your accounts the total of this column should equal the total of all the other expenditure columns added together.

Telephones	Car	Mailing	Books	Hospitality	Prof. M/ships	Pers. drawings	Total income	Inc: counselling
							£100.00	£100.00
			£20.00					
£80.00								
	£13.07							
			£14.98					
	£1.70							
£30.08								
							£50.00	£300.00
					£58.00			
	£129.23							
				£23.00				
		£100.00						
			£15.00				£54.00	
						£500.00		
£110.08	£144.00	£100.00	£49.98	£23.00	£58.00	£500.00	£204.00	£400.00
							Put all income in this column and then allocate it also to ONE other income column. When checking your accounts the total of this column should equal the total of all the other income columns added together.	Make additional Income columns as necessary, e.g. if you do training or supervision.

Employee confidentiality agreement

I _____ understand that during my employment with _____, whether this is as a volunteer, director or employee, I may be party to confidential information. I shall not during, or after termination of the engagement, disclose or allow the disclosure of any confidential information. The obligation of confidentiality both during and after the termination of this agreement shall not apply to any information which I am obliged to disclose under the Public Interest Disclosure Act 1998.

Any breach of this confidentiality agreement will automatically result in a disciplinary procedure and legal advice will be sought.

Signature ....

Date ....

Client information assessment form

Strictly confidential

Marital Status *Please circle as* *appropriate*	Single Engaged Married Living with a partner Separated Remarried Divorced Widowed
Sexuality *Please circle as* *appropriate*	Heterosexual Homosexual Lesbian Bisexual Other
Children *Please give the* *names and ages of* *all children,* *including any who* *have died. Indicate* *whether they are* *adopted or step-* *children*	
Occupation Present job: If you are unemployed, for how long? How long have you held this job? What jobs have you held during the last 10 years?	
Reason for seeking **help** What is the nature of your difficulties and how long have you been troubled by them? In what ways do you expect counselling to help you?	

What prompted you to seek help now?				

Family Information	Occupation	Present age	Age at death	Your age at that time
Father:				
Mother:				
Brothers and sisters: *(Please complete in birth order)*				

Your childhood
Please say something about your childhood

Education
Please give brief details of education and qualifications

Health
Have you had any serious illnesses or condition requiring hospitalisation?
If yes, please give dates and details.

Yes/No (please delete one reply).

Have you ever had psychiatric treatment?
If yes, please give dates and details.

Yes/No (please delete one reply).

Are you on medication for any condition? If yes, please say what it is and the condition.	**Yes/No** (please delete one reply).
GP information Name of GP GP's address GP's telephone number	
Further Information This form cannot cover every aspect of your life and some factors which you consider important may have been left out. Please use this space if you need to, and if necessary continue on another sheet, to tell me anything that you think I should know, such as difficulties at work, sexual problems, tensions in marital, social or work relationships.	

Client details and agreement form

Your personal details

Your full name	
Your home address, including post code	
Home phone number	
Work phone number	
Mobile phone number	
Email	
How do you prefer to be contacted?	
Your date of birth	

Your doctor's details Doctor's name	
Name of the general practice	
Address of the general practice	
Phone number	

My agreement

By signing below I agree that I have read and understood the Client Information Sheet that I have received, and that I agree to abide by the Terms and Conditions contained therein.

In addition, I give my permission for [PUT YOUR NAME HERE] to make contact with the appropriate agencies if he/she believes I am a danger to myself or to others.

Your signature: _____

Date: _____

Job application form

Can be found on resources section on www.karnacbooks.com

INDEX

Locators shown in *italics* refer to tables and forms.